FRANCESCO UBERTINI
CALLED
IL BACCHIACCA

FRANCESCO UBERTINI
CALLED
IL BACCHIACCA

BY LADA NIKOLENKO

J. J. AUGUSTIN PUBLISHER
LOCUST VALLEY, NEW YORK

1966
ALL RIGHTS RESERVED
LIBRARY OF CONGRESS CATALOGUE NUMBER 66–2377
PRINTED IN GERMANY BY J. J. AUGUSTIN, GLÜCKSTADT

TO

MY PATIENT HUSBAND

CONTENTS

Introduction 7

Stylistic Analysis and Chronology of Paintings by Bacchiacca 9

Catalogue Raisonné of the Authentic Paintings 33

Attributed Paintings 64

False Attributions 71

Lost Paintings 86

Copies after Bacchiacca 91

Bibliography 96

INTRODUCTION

F rancesco Ubertini called il Bacchiacca is a controversial figure among the Florentine Mannerists from the first half of the sixteenth century. It is regrettable that Giorgio Vasari did not devote a complete biography to him. However, he is mentioned in the Lives of Perugino, Pontormo, Granacci, Franciabigio, and Tribolo.[1] A somewhat more extensive description appears in the Life of Aristotele di San Gallo.[2] Vasari showed a condescending attitude towards Bacchiacca which was inherited, with few exceptions, by most of the art historians who ever wrote on this Florentine master. Vasari praised Bacchiacca's skill in painting small figures, especially animals, birds and plants. The emphasis on "small" pictures created an image of a typical "cassone" painter. The monumental compositions were later attributed to the more famous artists, and reassigned to Bacchiacca only with a certain reluctance. The establishment of Bacchiacca as an interesting and original, if somewhat ambiguous figure among Tuscan Mannerists, is the main purpose of this work.

The biographical data on Bacchiacca is scarce. Like many of his contemporary artists he was the son of a goldsmith.[3] His full name is Francesco di Ubertino (Ubertini) di Bartolomeo Verdi Filippini, and he was born in Borgo S. Lorenzo in Mugello near Florence on March 1, 1494. When Francesco was eleven years old, his father died. His elder brother, Bartolomeo detto Bacchio, who was born in 1484, was also a painter and the pupil of Perugino, but his artistic achievements remain a mystery which could hardly be

---

[1] Vasari, *Vite*, Vol. III, ed. Milanesi, 1878–82, p. 592; Vol. VI, p. 261, note 4; Vol. V, p. 343; Vol. V, p. 196; Vol. VI, p. 87.
[2] *Ibid.*, Vol. VI, pp. 443, 455–456.
[3] *Ibid.*, Vol. VI, p. 450, note 1.

solved by one work attributed to him—a drawing of Christ mentioned by Vasari in the life of Perugino. Bacchiacca's younger brother, Antonio, born in 1499, was an excellent weaver in the employ of Duke Cosimo I. His skill was praised by Benedetto Varchi in one of his sonnets.[4] Among their elder relatives were a notary and an apothecary, and Bacchiacca himself was admitted to the Guild of Physicians and Apothecaries in 1529.

Bacchiacca's first teacher was Perugino who had his work-shop in Florence around 1505–1506. It is fairly possible that he later went to Perugia with his brother Bartolomeo Bacchio. However, around 1514 he was again in Florence, and when Pope Leo X visited his native city in 1515, young Bacchiacca decorated the pontiff's residence, together with Pontormo, Ghirlandaio and Franciabigio.[5]

The assertion that Bacchiacca spent the later years of his apprenticeship with Franciabigio is probably based on the statement that: "Dopo qualche tempo dalla bottega del Perugino passo a quella del Francia".[6] They had been working together before Bacchiacca went to Rome and Franciabigio died in 1525. The melancholy elegance of Bacchiacca's late portraits, together with the precise execution of figures and the predilection for metallic blue, show his affinity with the art of Franciabigio.

Together with Andrea del Sarto, Pontormo and Granacci, Bacchiacca took part in the decoration of the bridal chamber of Giovan Francesco Borgherini. This was commissioned by his father, Salvi Borgherini, and was decorated with panels and exquisite furniture.[7]

This chamber at the Borgherini Palace in Borgo S. Apostolo was very famous in those days. In 1529, during the siege of Florence by the French, Giovanbattista della Palla, an art dealer, attempted to obtain the decorations in order to present them to the King of France. The indignant speech of the valiant Margareta Borgherini, so charmingly re-told by Vasari, shows how much these decorations were cherished by their owners. And yet a little more than fifty years later, in 1584, the heirs of Borgherini sold part of the panels

[4] F. Baldinucci, *Notizie de'Professori del Disegno*, Firenze, MDCCXXVIII, Dec. IV del Sec. 1530–1540, p. 290.

[5] L. Lanzi, *History of Painting in Italy*, 1828, I, p. 216.

[6] F. Canuti, *Il Perugino*, 1931, p. 279.

[7] Vasari, *Vite*, VI, p. 454.

and furniture to the Duke of Florence Francesco de'Medici for ninety ducats. The other part was inherited by the Sorbelli and Nerli families by marriage and sold at the beginning of the nineteenth century to Rev. J. Sanford, who obtained the two panels by Bacchiacca with the "Story of Joseph", which are now in the National Gallery, London.[8]

In 1525 Bacchiacca went to Rome. Not much is known of his life and activities there, except that he became a friend of Benvenuto Cellini,[9] and together they frequented the artists' club founded by the Sienese sculptor, Michelangelo di Bernardino di Michele, then engaged in the execution of the tomb of the late Pope Adrian VI.

The merry members of the club gathered at least twice a week. There Bacchiacca—a likeable and gregarious person—became acquainted with the already well-known pupils of Raphael, Giulio Romano and Francesco Penni. The half-amusing, half-scandalous episode of his love for the beautiful Roman courtesan, Pantasilea, was immortalized in an anecdote in the autobiography of Cellini.[10]

Bacchiacca came back to Florence before the catastrophe of the Sack of Rome. He married Tommasa di Carlo[11] and had three sons—Ubertino, Bastiano and Carlo. The latter became an artist, entirely unknown to posterity, a fate similar to that of his uncle, Bartolomeo Bacchio. It is possible that both, the brother and the son, were responsible for some of the weak works attributed to Bacchiacca.

From the end of the thirties until his death in 1557, Bacchiacca worked chiefly for the Duke of Florence, Cosimo de'Medici. Already in 1539,[12] he painted a part of the festive decorations for the wedding of the Duke to Eleonora of Toledo. In those lost paintings Bacchiacca glorified the Duke's ancestors—Cosimo the Elder, whom he painted returning from the exile, and Lorenzo the Magnificent arriving at Naples. Their emblems were doves and a pelican, probably masterfully executed. According to Vasari, it was his great

[8] B. Nicolson, "The Sanford Collection", *The Burlington Magazine*, July 1955, pp. 207–213.
[9] B. Cellini, *The Life...*, 1949, p. 50.
[10] *Ibid.*, p. 60.
[11] Vasari, *Vite*, VI, p. 450, note 1.
[12] *Ibid.*, VI, p. 87.

skill in this field which led Duke Cosimo to take him into his service. Around 1550–1551, or perhaps earlier, he was employed at the court with a salary of eight scudi a month.[13] The works of Bacchiacca for the ducal court were mainly of an ornamental character, including his well-known designs for tapestries of "The Months", and the "Groteschi"; frescos in the grotto of the newly-planned gardens of Palazzo Pitti; the ceiling decoration of the terrace adjoining the ante-room, and the triumphal arches for the festivities. The long lost "scrittoio", painted for the Duke with rare plants and birds of all kinds,[14] was at last found in the mezzanine between the first and the second floor overlooking the piazza.[15] Bacchiacca had also many commissions for paintings that were sent to France and England[16] and later attributed to more famous artists.

Bacchiacca's last work for the Medici comprised designs for a bed, which was used later as a wedding bed of Francesco de' Medici and Giovanna of Austria. These designs were replete with stories and little figures comparable to those painted before for the bridal chambers of the Florentine burgesses and as predellas of the large religious paintings executed by other artists. His brother, Antonio, had woven these little scenes and adorned them with pearls. And because Bacchiacca died before this sumptuous bed was finished, Maestro Giorgio Vasari, who had time for everything, completed the designs.

If we believe Vasari that Bronzino had painted the portrait of Bacchiacca, together with Pontormo and Gello, in his „Christ in Limbo",[17] he must be one of the three bearded men at the left, who, unfortunately, all look much alike. There is a fresco, painted by Vasari around 1556 in Palazzo Vecchio, that shows the Duke Cosimo surrounded by artists employed in his service. Between the profile of Bandinelli and the figure of the Duke, one sees, receding into the background, the face of an "unindentified artist".[18] It is again an image of an old bearded man and may possibly be a likeness of Francesco Ubertini called il Bacchiacca.

[13] F. M. Clapp, *Jacopo Carucci da Pontormo*, 1916, p. 184.
[14] Vasari, *Vite*, VI, p. 455.
[15] A. Lensi, *Palazzo Vecchio*, 1929, p. 136.
[16] Vasari, *Vite*, VI, pp. 455–456.
[17] *Ibid.*, VI, p. 456.
[18] B. Cellini, *The Life...*, p. 472, Notes ..., Frontispiece.

Giovanni Morelli,[19] who had studied Bacchiacca with considerable interest and found him "less known in the history of art than he deserves to be", expressed the hope that future art historians would someday create an historical portrait of him. Morelli was the first to enumerate in chronological order the paintings by Bacchiacca that he had discovered in the course of his artistic wanderings. He recognized Bacchiacca's talent and grace and at the same time did not deny his dependence upon his contemporary artists.

Bernard Berenson thought that Morelli overestimated the value of Bacchiacca's work.[20] Nevertheless he paid a very characteristic compliment to Bacchiacca by saying, "Although you will never discover in his pictures a figure positively his own, you will seldom find one positively out of place". The list of the works of Bacchiacca, compiled by Berenson, is short. Moreover, he seems to ignore a number of paintings now known, which may partially illustrate his disdain of the "petty" master.

He derided the "connoisseurs" who enjoyed Bacchiacca because of the ease with which they recognized his mannerisms. Berenson stated, however, that the Florentine artist had a "pretty vein of narrative, a certain simple charm of composition and a pleasant way of putting odds and ends together". In general, Berenson found Bacchiacca "not wholly contemptible even from an artistic standpoint". In any event, Bacchiacca has remained on the periphery of art history until the newly discovered works demanded a more penetrating study and re-evaluation.

A condescending benevolence persisted in the criticism on Bacchiacca to the present day. Italian art historians often added the adjective "poor" to his name, inspite of the fact that they did praise some of his works. Carlo Gamba[21] referred to Bacchiacca as "a crude and confused artist" while attributing to him "A Portrait of a Woman" at the Uffizi, which was formerly ascribed to Aurelio Luini.[22] He also assigned to him a "Holy Family" in the style of Vasari, calling it one of the artist's final aberrations.

[19] G. Morelli, *Critical Studies of Italian Painters*, 1900, pp. 101–113.
[20] B. Berenson, *Drawings of the Florentine Painters*, 1903, pp. 300–302.
[21] C. Gamba, "Nuove Attribuzioni di Ritratti", *Bolletino d'Arte*, 1924–25, IV, pp. 193–217.
[22] I do not discern Bacchiacca's hand from the study of this painting.

5

Adolfo Venturi[23] had stressed the poverty of fantasy in Bacchiacca and noticed the lack of mysticism in his "Deposition", while, at the same time, praising "The Girl with the Lute", "The Portrait of the Young Man", and the puerile grace he found in the depictions of Tobias.

Mario Tinti[24] published a booklet on Bacchiacca in his series "Piccola Collezione d'Arte" in 1925. He was the first to note Bacchiacca's fine draughtsmanship, his gift of observation, and his unconventional rendering of daily life. Emilio Cecchi[25] in 1929 wrote on two portraits—"The Girl with the Lute" and "Unknown Woman". The latter is now identified by Roberto Longhi as a work of Amico Friulano del Dosso.[26] In Cecchi's article, there appears the earliest reference to Bacchiacca as a Mannerist.

Early twentieth century art historians often did not approve of Bacchiacca's bright and smooth coloring. Hermann Voss[27] even denied his talent for composition but appreciated his bizarre fantasy. He found the type of women in Bacchiacca's paintings unpleasantly mannered and reproached him for the affectation in his drawings of hands and his treatment of draperies. Much deeper insight into Bacchiacca's art and personality was shown by N. Pevsner and O. Grautoff[28], W. Suida[29], and A. Scharf[30], who held the new ideas of Mannerism i.e. not as a decadent style, but as an expression of a new mental attitude in rebellion against the established ideal of the High Renaissance.[31] The "Saint Lawrence", (Fig. 78) published by Scharf, introduced the aspect of monumentality in Bacchiacca's work, which had not previously been associated with this artist.

[23] A. Venturi, *Storia dell'Arte Italiana*, 1925, IX, pp. 453–474.

[24] M. Tinti, *Il Bacchiacca*, 1925.

[25] E. Cecchi, "Dipinti del Bacchiacca", *Pinacotheca*, 1928–29, VII–VIII, pp. 88–92.

[26] R. Longhi, "L'Amico Friulano del Dosso", *Paragone*, No. 131, Nov. 1960, p. 7.

[27] H. Voss, *Spätmalerei der Renaissance in Rom und Florenz* 1920, p. 161.

[28] N. Pevsner—O. Grantoff, *Barockmalerei in den romanischen Ländern*, 1928, pp. 30–31.

[29] W. Suida, Leonardo und sein Kreis, 1929, p. 245.

[30] A. Scharf, "Bacchiacca: A New Contribution", *The Burlington Magazine*, 1937, pp. 60–70.

[31] W. Friedländer, "Die Entstehung des antiklassischen Stiles in der italienischen Malerei um 1520" *Repertorium für Kunstwissenschaft*, 1925, XLVI, p. 49.

In 1926, Arthur McComb published an article on Bacchiacca. His new listing consisted of fifty-seven paintings.[32] The largest amount of paintings was recorded by Roberto Salvini in Thieme-Becker "Künstlerlexicon" in 1933.[33]

Two interesting and lucid accounts on Bacchiacca have been written recently. One is the article by Luisa Marcucci[34] in the 1958 "Bolletino d'Arte", and the other a dissertation by Howard S. Merritt.[35] In her article Luisa Marcucci has noted a permanent lack of "terribilitá" in the michelagelesque works of Bacchiacca. She also suggested that it was perhaps due to this that Vasari did not write a biography of Bacchiacca. The author noted too the affinity with Piero di Cosimo as well as the influence of "forme nordiche" on the evolution of the artist's style.

Dr. Marcucci does not share the opinion of Siviero, the editor of the "Catalogue of the Second National Exhibition of the Works of Art Recovered in Germany",[36] who called Bacchiacca one of the best portrait painters of his time. Instead she finds an absence of psychological insight in his illustrative and provincial portraits. On the other hand, she thinks his landscapes important to the chronology of his works because of the increased space devoted to them in his later works. Characteristic of Bacchiacca is his development from his "maniera piccola" to his "maniera grande" with the transference of all details into a larger composition.

Dr. Merritt's work is primarily concerned with determining the influence of German engravings on the works of Bacchiacca. It is chiefly concentrated around works that illustrate this point, and nothing escapes Dr. Merritt's meticulous attention. The author's interest revolved around the discovery in Bacchiacca's works of traces of more significant paintings by well-known contemporaries. However, in the final analysis, Merritt too realized the limits of his subject as an artist, while at the same time, succombing to the

---

[32] A. McComb, "Bacchiacca", *The Art Bulletin*, 1926, VIII, pp. 141–167.

[33] R. Salvini, "Francesco Ubertini", *Thieme-Becker Lexicon*, 1939, XXXIII, pp. 522–523.

[34] L. Marcucci, "Contributo al Bacchiacca", *Bolletino d'Arte*, 1958, XLIII, pp. 26–39.

[35] Howard S. Merritt, *Bacchiacca Studies: The Use of Imitation*, Princeton, 1958.

[36] Siviero, ed. *Catalogue of the Second National Exhibition of the Works of Art Recovered in Germany*, 1950, Pls. 40–42.

peculiar charm of Bacchiacca's personality. In fact, most Bacchiacca criticism concludes with the realization of the master as an immensely appealing person, rather than as a problematic and significant artist.

Despite the scarcity of literature on Bacchiacca his paintings have appeared frequently in private collections, in museums, and at auctions throughout the many years. Perhaps this gradual recognition, without the fanfare of critics, is significant inasmuch as it demonstrates his appeal to the eye. He has slowly charmed students of cinquecento painting, as well as art collectors, and together with other Mannerists, is now enjoying unprecedented popularity.

Bacchiacca waited four hundred and four years for a kind of his "one-man show", which was presented by The Baltimore Museum of Art,[37] and entitled "Bacchiacca and his Friends". This is a challenging title considering that Pontormo, Andrea del Sarto, Vasari and others were grouped as "friends" around the controversial Bacchiacca. It was a rare occasion to see so many of his paintings at one time. It was also startling to realize that gathered together and surrounded by the paintings of his contemporaries Bacchiacca's works show that this somewhat enigmatic imitator was a distinctive personality, and that he lost nothing of his own character and originality when confronted with his more eminent cohorts. The exhibit was a tribute to all who concerted their efforts to present and explain Bacchiacca's work to others.

[37] *Bacchiacca and his Friends*, Catalogue of an Exhibition Presented by The Baltimore Museum of Art, Jan. 10–Febr. 19, 1961.

STYLISTIC ANALYSIS AND CHRONOLOGY OF
PAINTINGS BY BACCHIACCA

The establishment of a chronology for the paintings of Bacchiacca is indeed a difficult task. Giovanni Morelli's[1] divi-
sion of his artistic oeuvre into three periods is too con-
strictive for an artist who not only transferred parts of his own
compositions from painting to painting, but constantly adapted
themes and details from the works of other masters. Borrowings from
German engravings and contemporary paintings are evident
throughout his work and provide a fertile field for conjecture and
attribution. The only known dates of his paintings help to reveal,
however, the somewhat zig-zag line of his stylistic development. The
early Peruginesque period embraces the years between 1505 and
1515 and shows his complete dependence on his Umbrian teacher.
From the time of the panels with the Story of Joseph, between 1515
and 1518, dates the consolidation of this characteristic blend of
Florentine influences and borrowings from the Northern engravings
that persisted in his works throughout many years especially in his
landscapes. The period, introduced by his stay in Rome in 1525,
shows his new relish in feminine images. The unusual portrait of
the philosopher Salecchi, dated 1533, demonstrates a strong
Northern quality also reflected in his *Christ before Pilate* (Fig. 60),
the *Agony in the Garden* (Fig. 61) and the Madonna and Child with
the Infant Saint John in the Wiesbaden Gallery (Fig. 63). The
last and the less known period of his delayed maturity from the
forties until his death in 1557, based on michelangelesque and
vasaresque influences, reveal the development of his own monumentality. But the relapses into the former habit of copying and
repeating himself and the others are there and present new enigmas.
And yet Bacchiacca remains a noteworthy artist—and one cannot

[1] G. Morelli, *Critical Studies of Italian Painters*, 1900, pp. 104–113.

9

fail to appreciate the graceful harmony of his design, the strength of his line and his prominent, decorative color-scheme.

Certain characteristics of Bacchiacca should be considered in studying his work: the uneven quality of his paintings as manifest in works ranging from the very charming to the very naive and clumsy, and in the motifs hastily assembled from different paintings into a new creation; the preponderance of the visual rather than the spiritual, and finally the artist's own idiosyncracies which account, in part, for the playful, whimsical tone of his pictures.

Bacchiacca embarked on his artistic career in the studio of Perugino. His *Resurrection* (Fig. 1) in Dijon Museum, derived from his master's composition, and two paintings at the Christ Church in Oxford—*Noli me tangere* (Fig. 2) and *The Preaching of Christ* (Fig. 3) are examples of this early period. The *Descent from the Cross*, in the Museo Civico in Bassano, (Fig. 4), also assigned to the School of Perugino, belongs to this group of works. It has been pointed out by Oskar Fischel that the source for this composition was the now-ruined fresco by Perugino in S. Maria dei Servi in Citta della Pieve.[2] There are three variations of this painting, which were formerly all attributed to Bacchiacca. Only one of them, now in the Uffizi, is considered undoubtedly his work. The other one, in Pinacotheca Manfredini in Venice is attributed to Puligo. It is interesting, however that in spite of various changes in the three compositions, the two figures hurrying away with the dead body of one of the thieves remain constant. They are not contained in Perugino's fresco. The possible archtype of all these compositions, the *Deposition* modello from the workshop of Sansovino, shows one of the thieves hanging dead from the ladder on the left.[3] The kneeling man receives the corpse of the other thief on his shoulder. The men carrying away the dead seem to be Bacchiacca's own invention. Their marked haste contrasts with the statically poised figures about the Cross and the flutter of their loin-cloths is suggestive of mannerist striving towards picturesque restlessness. Herein, too, is an example of Bacchiacca's penchant for story-telling.

The *Descent from the Cross* (Fig. 35), in the Uffizi, still contains

[2] O. Fischel, *Die Zeichnungen der Umbrer*, 1917, p. 61.
[3] U. Middeldorf, "Sull'attività della bottega di Jacopo Sansovino", *Rivista d'Arte*, 8, 1936, pp. 259–260.

Peruginesque figures against a landscape which, though derived from different German prints, became an integral part of Bacchiacca's world. The position of the motifs in the painting might vary, but the vocabulary itself remains essentially the same—e.g. a group of trees with heavy foliage, the grey mountains, the white building with an arched entrance, small bushes and rocks in the foreground. Minor details, however, animate the composition in the Uffizi, such as the leaping white dog on the path on the right and the procession of horsemen wearing turbans and broad-rimmed hats. The head of Mary Magdalen standing to the left of the Cross has a gentle Umbrian quality. Her subtle almost leonardesque smile appears again in a group of later Madonnas in the several compositions depicting the Virgin with Saint Anne and Saint Elisabeth and the Infant St. John.

Returning from Umbria to Florence at the age of eighteen, Bacchiacca was subjected to many influences—that of Andrea del Sarto, Franciabigio, Fra Bartolomeo and Albertinelli. His talent, uneven and unstable, always blossomed in the shadow of a greater personality, imbibing its influence with astonishing ease unhampered by excessive ambition or a feeling of rivalry. But he retained much from Perugino—i.e. his lack of the inventive power and also something of his spiritual calm. The new influences, however, were at work when he executed *Scenes from the Life of Joseph* for Borgherini's chamber, small brightly colored panels, crowded with "figure piccole".[4] Vasari has spoken of those so often that it seems sometimes as if Bacchiacca had never painted anything else. The agitated figures fill the two long panels in the National Gallery in London (Figs. 8–9) and a series of scenes in the Borghese Gallery in Rome (Figs. 10–13). Some of the figures may be found in other paintings: the affected boy appears again in two "Baptism of Christ", one in the Berlin Museum and the other in the Vassar College Art Gallery. The angry half-nude man with the fantastic head-gear, at the extreme left of one of the London panels, recalls the figure of a soldier in the *Flagellation* in the National Gallery in Washington D.C. (Fig. 83). Gnoli and Borenius[5] once rightly

[4] G. Vasari, *Vite*, V, p. 343.
[5] T. Borenius, *Catalogue of the Collection of Sir Herbert Cook in Richmond at Doughty House*, 1913, I, p. 63, No. 54.

attributed the Washington painting to Bacchiacca. The figure which personifies Mary Magdalen in the Uffizi *Descent from the Cross*, appears again in the "Life of Joseph" standing under the arch of the central, Peruginesque building, reminiscent of the one in the *Preaching of Christ* in Oxford and in the *Legend of the Dead King* in the Dresden Gallery.

The series of paintings depicting the story of Adam and Eve and their children belong to Bacchiacca's early Umbro-florentine period and reveal a blend of influences. A small composition, *Adam and Eve* (Fig. 7) in the Johnson Collection in Philadelphia had been attributed to Giulio Romano as well as to Peruzzi before Morelli's acuteness discovered the amazing transformation to which Bacchiacca subjected Perugino's work "Apollo and Marsyas". With his teacher's cartoon as a starting point, he turned Apollo into Eve and Marsyas into Adam. The face of Eve remained that of Apollo while the broad-shouldered figure became more feminine. Her two children are with her, and her body is partially masked by a cloak. The figure of Adam is heavier more masculine than that of Marsyas, with its long hair and beard. Instead of the warm Umbrian landscape of Perugino Bacchiacca placed Adam and Eve against a dark forest more akin to Dürer's engraving of the same subject. A wall of trees, with golden brown trunks and dark foliage complete the background. Graceless anatomical details are softened by the exquisite coloration—cool grey flesh tones against darkly gleaming trees. The violet-tinted blue of the cloak of Eve appears later in many of Bacchiacca's scarfs and mantles.

Some years later, when his drawing became more certain and his coloring more delicate, Bacchiacca again used the figures of Eve and her children—e.g. the small *Caritas* (Fig. 25) in the Metropolitan Museum of Art in New York. The lovely landscape is an amalgam of different borrowings. It is enlivened by a group of deers in the distance, while a parrot, directly derived from Dürer's engraving, is perched on the twig. Hardly a shadow appears on faces and bodies among the bluish tones of this very smooth panel.

Also connected with Adam and Eve story is the *Creation of Eve* (Fig. 16), formerly in the New Palace, Potsdam. It is almost a copy of Fra Bartolomeo's composition in the Seattle Art Museum. Giuseppe Fiocco has noted the dependence of Fra Bartolomeo's painting

12

on a composition attributed to Raphael in a private collection in Sweden.[6] Bacchiacca introduced a group of trees, rocks, hills and ample clouds in the sky into his variation of this composition which stress the Northern character of the painting. It might be of somewhat later date than *Adam and Eve* in Philadelphia, probably painted around 1518, and earlier than *Caritas* executed ca. 1523. Unfortunately Bacchiacca's version disappeared in 1945, but one can see from the photograph that he repeated the figures in the composition faithfully, if not skilfully. Later he even used the figure of God in this painting as a model for the Moses in the *Gathering of Manna* (Fig. 71) in the National Gallery, Washington D. C.

The picture *Cain Slaying Abel* (not illustrated) listed among the doubtful attributions, is in the opinion of Adolfo Venturi, an example of collaboration of Albertinelli and Bacchiacca. The gesture of Cain violently lifting his club, the touching effeminate figure of Abel, the frightened shepherd at the right have none of the rigidity of Bacchiacca's personages. The raven pilfering the basket placed on the ground is a note of the genre more characteristic of Bacchiacca than of Albertinelli. Such genre touches were to become more pronounced in his work with the years.

Another odd touch has been added to the composition *Christ Carrying the Cross* (Fig. 6) in the collection of Mr. John Drury-Lowe in Derbyshire, England. Here too one marks the blend of peruginesque features and the colors of Bacchiacca characteristic of the early compositions around 1520. The stiff folds of the mantle, the auburn hair of Christ, His hands, inactively folded over the cross, still point out to Perugino's influence. However, the scene in the background is more typical of the simple man from the Mugello Valley. St. Antony Abbot is seen unhurriedly walking behind a trotting ass laden with burden. A peasant, carrying a mattock over his shoulder, heads the procession while a pig brings up the rear. The whole company marches along, without paying much attention to the tragedy in the foreground.

In fact Bacchiacca was often more successful with staffage elements which appear in the backgrounds of his paintings than with the more monumental biblical and allegorical figures in the fore-

[6] G. Fiocco, "Fra Bartolomeo e Raffaello", *Rivista d'Arte*, XXIX, 1954, pp. 43–53.

ground. He was continually finding some new species—a bird, a squirrel, a gazelle—to adorn his compositions. Though often directly adapted from the works of others, these animated creatures seem to enter his designs with the greatest ease gaining much in color and spriteliness.

In the case of the tondo *Ghismonda with the Heart of Guiscardo* (Fig. 17), formerly called the *Crystal-Gazing Scene* in the Kress Collection, Bacchiacca's originality is not disputed because of the unique subject, striking colors and a somewhat clumsy grace of the figures. This composition, dated about 1520–21, is also close to the *Young Lute Player* (Fig. 39) painted about 1522–23. This is a portrait of a young man, lute in hands, seated on a parapet in front of a landscape bathed in a romantic mood. He has a wistful look and the hourglass, which stands on the parapet on the left, seems to measure the slow passage of time. The unpleasant harsh tone of his violet-pink garment with green sleeves is most probably due to overcleaning. This picture is related to a still more interesting one, the *Portrait of the Old Man* (Fig. 40) in the Cassel Museum. Dr. Schmidt-Degener has identified it as a portrait of Pope Adrian VI which Bacchiacca painted after the sculptured effigy of the Pontiff.[7] This was erected on his tomb by the Sienese sculptor, Michelangelo di Bernardino di Michele, a leading force in the artistic circle in Rome, of which Bacchiacca was one of the members. Michelangelo di Michele executed this monument together with Tribolo in 1524. Bacchiacca could have seen it in 1525 when he was in Rome. If this emaciated old man in monastic garb, holding a skull, is the Pope Adrian VI, Bacchiacca could have painted this postumous portrait only after 1525. Although the portrait is of later date than the *Young Lute Player*, the two paintings are analogous in composition and in atmosphere. In both is featured the hourglass—symbol of time's irrevocable course—and the Triumphs of Love and Death. Bacchiacca was not very subtle in his use of symbols—e.g. the Triumph of Love in the background on the right as accompaniment to the figure of the young man. Daphne and Apollo in the middle distance—a tribute to mythology—show a slender youth kneeling at the feet of a figure whose raised arms are turning into twigs. The

[7] F. Schmidt-Degener, "About the Bacchiacca's Portrait of an Old Man", *The Burlington Magazine*, 1939, 74, pp. 234–239.

other couple of famous lovers—Samson and Dalilah—this time a biblical subject, dressed in the contemporary fashion, are seen at the left. The ability of Bacchiacca to blend contradictory elements into a harmonious whole is fully demonstrated by this painting.

The *Old Man* or the *Pope Adrian VI* has received his Triumph of Death—the lot of the aged. The gloomy allegory is placed in front of the white building which appears in different pictures of Bacchiacca with the strange insistence of a dream. Both portraits are essentially romantic, although the treatment of the Old Man's face is stronger and more mature than that of the Young Lute Player. The triumphs of love and death are adapted from the Florentine engravings of the fifteenth century.

Stories from the Old Testament, such as Adam and Eve and their progeny, Moses, the young Tobias, were favorite subjects for festive decorations on the Day of St. John the Baptist, patron saint of Florence. The apocryphal story of Tobias and the Angel was often commissioned by parents of young voyagers. The typical depiction of Tobias as a timid boy rather than an enterprising young traveller particularly suited Bacchiacca whose art has a soft albeit feminine inclination.[8] His Tobias and the Angel is a touching expression to anxious mothers awaiting their sons.

One of his best Tobias pictures is in the Wadsworth Atheneum in Hartford, Connecticut (Fig. 33). The young Tobias, looking quite effeminate dressed in pale blue, holding his right hand against his chest, kneels before the Angel who is garbed in pink and yellow with a pair of large blue-brown wings. In a similar painting, formerly in the collection of Dr. Simon in Berlin (Fig. 34), a very similar Tobias kneels in like manner before the Angel wearing a wreath upon his saintly head like a mythological figure of a Muse. Bacchiacca's Tobias not only follow the Angel, but kneels before him in veneration, although it was only at the end of his journey that his kinsman revealed himself as his celestial guardian. The landscape in both paintings is that peculiar "land of Bacchiacca". Another version, now in the Uffizi (Fig. 15), shows a still younger Tobias. Here is a little boy, dressed in the Florentine fashion of the day, looking up to the Angel who is shrouded in a crimson mantle.

[8] G. Coor-Achenbach, "The Iconography of Tobias and the Angel in the Florentine Painting of the Renaissance", *Marsyas*, 1946, 3, pp. 72–73.

Historians of art mention still another interpretation of the Tobias in the Troyes Museum which appears to be an old catalogue's error. The Troyes Museum possesses neither the painting nor any records concerning it.[9]

Bacchiacca's works falls into groups. One of them includes three variations on the theme of *St. John the Baptist in the Wilderness*. The one of the three small paintings is in the Museum of the Bob Jones University in South Carolina (Fig. 26). According to Dr. E. Tietze-Conrat, this panel was a section of wainscot from the Borgherini Chamber.[10] In this painting of St. John, Bacchiacca used the pose of the seated Adam from the composition of the *Creation of Eve*. Mottled deers animate the left foreground, while in the larger and later version in the Bremen Museum (Fig. 51) a squirrel, two birds and a gazelle lend fresh charm to the painting. The pose of the Saint is different too and the rendering of the anatomy more skilfull. The third painting, slightly changed by different details, is in the Newhouse Galleries in New York (Fig. 27).

The warm, strongly tinted coloring of St. John's body in all three paintings contrasts with Bacchiacca's usual treatment of it in pearly greenish grey highlighted with pale pink tints. The warm brown of the foliage is in harmony with the golden and brown hair of the Saint and the skin of the deers.

Two long panels, probably for cassoni, were painted for the Benintendi family about 1523. One of these, *The Legend of the Dead King* (Fig. 28) in the Dresden Gallery is indeed unusual in composition. Bacchiacca's fantastic if limited world is here seen at its best. The subject of the panel is taken from "Gesta Romanorum", a collection of moralized fables dated from the early fourteenth century. Bacchiacca used the mediaeval version of the story in which King Solomon appears neath the porch surrounded by his suite. At his side is a full-armored knight carrying a banner adorned with the double-headed eagle of Byzantine emperors. The figure of the Dead King is similar to that of Christ, while the nude man behind him is apparently another victim being led to execution. However, it is doubtful that Bacchiacca penetrated all the theo-

[9] Letter of the Director of the Troyes Museum, France, dated 1/28/1960.
[10] E. Tietze-Conrat, *The Bob Jones Collection of Religious Paintings, Bob Jones University, Greenville, South Carolina* Catalogue, 1954, Pl. 53.

logical subleties of the Christian variation of this tragic tale very deeply.[11] He was again not inventive in his figures using the same nude man already represented in the scene of the baptism in his predella with the *Scenes from the Life of St. Acasio* (Figs. 21–22–23), which he painted in 1521. The legitimate son, who refuses to shoot an arrow into his father's body and inherit the kingdom, is in the center near the steps of the building. He has thrown aside his bow and arrow and pathetically presses his right hand against his chest. One immediately recognizes the young Tobias, with his softly moulded features, his hair combed back, his dangling plumed hat, his reverential pose. Even his white dog with the bushy tail is here again sniffing at the ground in a manner comparable to that in the pictures of Tobias and the Angel probably executed around the same time. The landscape is bizarre and vivid, dominated by full-blown white clouds.

Like *The Legend of the Dead King*, the *Baptism of Christ* (Fig. 29) in the Berlin Museum comes from the Palazzo Benintendi in Florence. It is a long panel with several figures, grouped on the banks of the little brook against grey rocks and trees. The heavy foliage is painted in layers commensurate with the German engravings from which they are derived and quite different from the slender, transparent Umbrian trees of his earlier landscapes. Several men, preparing themselves for baptism, are situated in the left background. The lower torso of one of the figures is very similar to that of the man being led to execution in *The Legend of the Dead King*. Another man let his attendand to help him pull off his stockings. With his sharp eye for details Bacchiacca caught the gesture of people moving about him and painted them in his quick, easy way.

As usual, Bacchiacca has repeated the composition of Baptism several times with slight variations. The central group of Christ and St. John is similar in the picture in Berlin and that in the Vassar College Art Gallery (Fig. 36). The small painting of the same subject, formerly in the Mond Collection (Fig. 37) shows the central group directly adapted from Perugino while the figures repeated from Bacchiacca's compositions the *Story of Joseph* and *St. Acasio* predella are placed on both sides in the foreground. *The Baptism*

[11] W. Stechov, "Shooting at Father's Corpse", *The Art Bulletin*, 1942, 24, p. 220.

in the Vassar College Art Gallery is intense in color. Particularly notable is the unpleasantly bright blue of the sky again caused by the removal of the fine red glazings with which Bacchiacca achieved the lovely lilac and greenish shade of this color. All compositions of the Baptism still belong to the time previous to Bacchiacca's trip to Rome, a turning point of his artistic activity.

During his stay in Rome in 1525, Bacchiacca met many artists and women and ,enjoyed the brief but most colorful period of his life. The response to the lure of the feminine is the strongest and most ingenuous aspect of Bacchiacca's talent. Influenced by the famous composition of Leonardo—*Leda and the Swan*—he created a series of small paintings of this subject (Figs. 43–44–45–46–47). His Ledas almost have the indecent charm of Folies Bergères girls. Bacchiacca destroyed the dignity of their nudity by giving them but the slightest attire—veils, coifs, jewels, and sandals—the practice adapted by the Fontainebleu School. Only the pale blond Leda in the collection of Mr. and Mrs. Linsky in New York (Fig. 45) is innocently nude, but ridiculously posed on the back of an enormous swan, she is not too dissimilar from the other Ledas. Bacchiacca's portraits of ladies demonstrate his almost timid admiration of feminine beauty and the richness of their attire. They are by no means psychological studies, but neither are they merely variation on a theme. Bacchiacca dressed the yellow and auburn hair of his women with infinite care; he adorned them lavishly with jewels and gave them flowers, pets, and precious vessels.

Among the female portraits is one which could be tentatively called the "portrait of Pantasilea", his scandalous Roman mistress. It is a small painting of Magdalen in the Palazzo Pitti (Fig. 48). Despite the unrealistic costume and the sibyllic head-gear, typical of the circle of Michelangelo, this face retains an intensity of a living memory. It conforms to the character of this woman as outlined by Cellini—deceitful, careless, elusive. It is one of the best works of Bacchiacca, his own little "Mona Lisa", reduced in quality and significance, but delightful in color and sophisticated in expression. Like many pictures of women with an enigmatic smile it had been formerly attributed to the school of Leonardo.[12] Here is

[12] O. H. Giglioli, "Notiziario—R. Galleria Pitti", *Rivista d'Arte*, 1909, 6, p. 150.

the elongated face, with a pointed chin and bold dark eyes under the high-raised eye-brows which appear to be plucked and drawn with an eye-brow pencil. Her hairdo with rows of round locks and two small braids is often repeated in other paintings. The cool transparent tone of her face with an olive-green shadow on her left cheek and temple contrasts with the glowing red of her garment formed by layers of light glazings. Her long sleeves are trimmed with leopard fur, a broad collar of the same fur covers her shoulders leaving her long neck exposed. Her face appears light and smooth against the dark-green background. She holds an agate vase—the classic attribute of Magdalen—in her hands with typical wide outstretched thumb and forefinger, but her mien is by no means repentant. She casts a sidewise glance, drawing up the corners of her lips in an imperceptible smile, which Adolfo Venturi calls archaic.[13] However, this very smile could also have been on the lips of Pantasilea when she sat together with other women at the table of the merry host, Michelangelo di Michele.

Woman with the Cat (Fig. 50) in a private collection in Italy again has "Pantasilea's" face. Her attire, reminiscent of Michelangelo, is seen on several figures of Bacchiacca's later period, after 1525. It is a dress with a square neck line and two round agraffes, a crescent-shaped coif over the familiar hairdo with small hanging braids. She holds in her hands a cat, which gracefully crosses her paws on her mistress's breast, making the picture appear both fantastic and intimate. The reddish fur of the cat is echoed in the auburn hair of the woman, establishing a closer physical relationship between the two. Even if it is a "tactile allegory", as it has been suggested,[14] it remains, first and foremost, an image of a woman with a cat. This somewhat banal, but unvariably fascinating combination has been transmitted to other "poets of the flesh" including Renoir with his *Girl with a Cat*.

"Pantasilea" appears several times in Bacchiacca's paintings. The little Cupid in the curious *Portrait of a Courtesan* (Fig. 49) formerly in the Remak Collection in Berlin,[15] has the same face, slightly changed

[13] A. Venturi, *Storia dell'arte italiana*, 1925, 9, p. 470.

[14] *Catalogue of the Exhibition—Le Triumphe du Mannerisme Européen de Michelange au Greco*. Amsterdam, July 1st-Oct. 19, 1955, pp. 48–49.

[15] I. Berge, "Un dipinto sconosciuto del Bacchiacca e il suo modello", *Rivista d'Arte*, 1935, XVII, p. 85.

by a broader and more childish smile. This portrait, now called the *Portrait of a Lady and Child* in the University Galleries, University of Southern California, is an interesting example of the Roman reminiscences of Bacchiacca. The lovely young woman holds a purse in her hands while Cupid pulls its strings—a very clear symbolization of venal love—certainly appropriate for Bacchiacca, who was hardly a master of mysterious devices. This painting is done after a drawing attributed at times to Michelangelo, to his pupil Andrea, to Antonio Mini, and even to Bacchiacca. He could have copied it when he was in Rome and later used in this somewhat eccentric portrait, probably executed in the late twenties.

These feminine likenesses are very different from the earlier one, the stiff and very dignified *Lady with a Nosegay* in the Isabella Stewart Gardner Museum in Boston (Fig. 41). The line of her neck, adorned with a golden chain, and her shoulders repeat the lines in the *Portrait of Lucrezia del Fede* by Andrea del Sarto in Prado, which for some unknown reason is attributed to Bacchiacca by Ingeborg Fraenkel in her book "Andrea del Sarto.[16] The face of the woman in the Prado has nothing in common with most of Bacchiacca's feminine types. The modeling of her features is so characteristic of Andrea, so soft and painterly, that this comparison may well demonstrate the principle difference between the two artists, i.e. the stiffness and sharp outline in Bacchiacca as compared to the softness and mellow blend of lines and colors by Andrea.

The extremely interesting and almost unknown *Portrait of a Pilosopher Origene Salecchi* (Fig. 57) is dated 1533. It reveals a combination of a strong Northern character acquired through the steady use of German engravings and of features derived from his more gifted contemporaries—Pontormo and Bronzino. In his *Portrait of a Philosopher* Bacchiacca captured the steady, somber gaze, so characteristic of Pontormo, and something of Bronzino's rigid and impassive elegance. In the portraits of women,[17] however, he retained his own weakness for rich garments and lovely, delicate details—witness the pale crystal flower at the right temple of the *Girl with a Lute* (Fig. 56) in the collection of the Count Contini-

[16] I. Fraenkel, *Andrea del Sarto*, 1935, pp. 100–102.
[17] C. Gamba, "Nuove Attribuzioni di Ritratti", *Bolletino d'Arte*, 1924/25, 4, p. 193.

Bonacossi in Florence. This picture has elicited praise, even from Adolfo Venturi, who, like most of the Italian art historians, was not very amiable to Bacchiacca. But for this portrait he found words of admiration pointing out its "contradiction of defects in form and a fine quality in decorative effect".[18] The *Girl with a Lute* is executed in large strongly colored masses which contrasts with the cassone-like details in the background. She has a strange very light face with thinly drawn eyebrows, watchful dark eyes and a firm, serious mouth. Her head, enlarged by a dark turban, is prominent against the pale sky. Her voluminous violet-pink sleeves recall the *Portrait of a Young Lute Player*, and make her "arthritic" hands apper even smaller. There are cast shadows under her nose, on her cheek and throat, unthinkable in Bacchiacca's earlier works. As this painting represents a commissioned portrait, few jewels are worn.

Bacchiacca was, like others, impressed by greatness and complexity of Michelangelo's art, but being neither great nor complex, he imitated only his outward forms, his noble poses, his proud profiles and his powerful bodies. Gradually he acquired his own "grand" manner, sometimes amusing, sometimes incongruous because of the introduction of monumental michelangelesque figures into his smaller world. The new personages had met the old ones and had become peacefully integrated. An example of this type of painting is his *Decapitation of St. John the Baptist* in Berlin (Fig. 69). Detlev von Hadeln recognized the derivation from Dürer's woodcut *Salome with the Head of St. John.*[19] The large group of old friends is put compactly into a landscape of earlier times. It is unnecessary to enumerate the details for they remain the same, but Salome is a new michelangelesque figure, with a pensive and noble face under her white head-gear. Quite statuesque, she holds her plate as a dancer would hold her tambourine. The courtesan from the Roman portrait and slyly smiling "Pantasilea" peeping out from between two women are the maids. The clear, distinct colors are perhaps not in harmony with this grim scene, but they are indigenous to Bacchiacca, who always was an artist of colors for colors' sake.

[18] A. Venturi, *Storia dell'Arte Italiana*, 1925, 9, p. 464.
[19] D. v. Hadeln, "Bilder Romaninos und Bacchiaccas und ihre Beziehung zu Dürer", *Jahrbuch d. kön. Preuß. Kunstsammlung*, 1908, 29, pp. 247–251.

This painting had been executed between 1535 and 1545 and demonstrates the characteristics of Bacchiacca's later period.

The same dancing Salome appears in the midst of one of the most interesting paintings of Bacchiacca's mature period—*The Gathering of Manna* in the National Gallery, Washington D. C. (Fig. 71). Together with *Moses Striking the Rock* (Fig. 70), formerly in the Prince Giovanelli Collection in Venice, these two paintings probably belonged to the story of Moses mentioned by Vasari among the works of Bacchiacca.[20] *Moses Striking the Rock* was formerly considered the work of Dürer. Once a compliment, this is now a reproach of plagiarism. It has not been possible to trace the present whereabouts of this painting but the coloring in *the Gathering of Manna* might give some indication as to the color scheme here. The blues and greens of the landscape even recall some of the distant views of Patinir.

Both pictures are crowded with animals, wild and domestic, huddled in one spot, waiting for food and water. The exotic giraffe (taken from Piero di Cosimo) is introduced next to placid looking cows. The small white rabbit in the Washington painting does not seem to be frightened by its proximity to the wild spotted beasts— demonstrating a set of laws operative for the artistic animal kingdom different from the laws of nature.[21] The influence of Northern engravings and woodcuts is striking in these two paintings, but the friendly and peaceful atmosphere of Bacchiacca prevails. Vasari, in speaking of Pontormo, reproached him for his adaption of "maniera tedesca" rather than for his borrowings from the German masters.[22] The mannerism of Bacchiacca did not absorb the troubled spirit and anguish of the new art that terminated the classic era. For at the time of the death of Raphael and the protest of Luther, marking the end of the golden age of the Renaissance, Bacchiacca was still young and placidly Umbrian in spirit. He had become a mannerist in his own fashion. And, as usual, he was at his best in the paintings with genre touches and his images of women and far less successful in compositions filled with men, horses and action,

[20] G. Vasari, *Vite*, VI, p. 452.
[21] H. Friedman, "Bacchiacca's Gathering of Manna in the National Gallery", *Gazette des Beaux-Arts*, 1947, 31/32, p. 158.
[22] G. Vasari, *Vite*, VI, p. 270.

like his *Conversion of St. Paul* (Fig. 74) in the Rochester Memorial Art Gallery and his *Martyrs of the Ararat* in Florence (Fig. 75).

The *Conversion of St. Paul*, important as "Michelangelo document", has been masterfully analysed by Merritt.[23] This conglomeration of unnaturally short figures, gesticulating in a clumsy fashion, and of carousel-like horses is unalleviated by Bacchiacca's own style. The task was too difficult for him. Harsh colors are perhaps due to disappearance of the glazings, or perhaps Vasari's works absorbed too much of Bacchiacca's attention at this time. Merritt's idea that the horseman on the left is Bacchiacca himself is appealing, for the grinning face is quite different from the surrounding masks.

The *Martyrs of the Ararat* in the S. Felippo Neri Chapel in the Church of S. Firenze, Florence can hardly be seen now, so covered is it by dirt, darkened varnish and long cracks. Its composition is better organized than the *Conversion of St. Paul*. The figures are more elegant than in the latter painting, the faces have more character and vigor. One feels that the colors must have been strong, stressing the violence of the scene. But even in this late and mature period, Bacchiacca could not refrain from his habit of repeating figures from his earlier compositions. The prostrated corpse from his *Descent from the Cross* and the groveling man from the two Moses pictures are seen, united in a group, in the background on the left. The profile of a bearded man, presenting prisoners to King Sapor, could be seen at the extreme left in the *Conversion of St. Paul*. The *Martyrs of the Ararat* must be of later date, for the entire painting reflects a more mature style, a new seriousness.

The large panel *Saint Lawrence* (Fig. 78), probably a right wing of a triptych, once in the New Palace in Potsdam but location unknown since 1945, may be studied at present by means of a photograph.[24] It is interesting to notice how Bacchiacca interrupts the large form of the Saint's figure by painting miniature reproductions of his own works as embroidered details on the cassock, e.g. the Dresden Madonna (Fig. 72) is clearly recognizable, although partially altered. The other embroideries on the sleeves and about the draped cloak may be copies of other works no longer extant.

[23] H. S. Merritt, *Bacchiacca Studies; The Use of Imitation*, Princeton, 1958.
[24] Letter from *Verwaltung der Staatlichen Schlösser und Gärten*, Potsdam-Sanssouci, 12/22/1959.

Bacchiacca celebrated his private "Triumph of Mannerism" in his picture: *Lady with a Vase of Flowers* (Pl. 76) in the Springfield Museum of Fine Arts. Together with *The Florentine Street Scene* in the Rijksmuseum, Amsterdam (Fig. 80), this painting was shown in 1955 at the exhibition entitled "Le Triumphe du Mannerisme Europeen de Michelange au Greco". *Lady with the Vase of Flowers* is michelangelesque but softened by Bacchiacca's peculiar grace and the refinement of costume. In her dress and head-cloth blue once more mingles with lilac, yellow with red. She is lavishly adorned with jewels—two necklaces, brooches, a bracelet. One instinctively senses the pleasure which the artist must have derived in painting all this—her skilfully arranged turban, its line repeated by the yellow hair covering heavily her ears, with stylized braids descending on her throat. This Lady would indeed be quite at home in a painting of the Fontainebleu School, but for her somewhat melancoly expression, whereby the artist has succeeded in obtaining a real personal likeness of his subject. Although a purely decorative figure—all art and style—the Madonna in The Baltimore Museum of Art (Fig. 66) bears a strong resemblance to her. Bacchiacca was influenced by the majestic and impersonal type of Michelangelo's women, but he was too far from abstraction, too close to living people, too quick to grasp the characteristics of a human face, to be merely an imitator. Instead of the idealized form of Michelangelo, one finds a Florentine contemporary transformed into a Madonna or an allegoric figure. A similarity of this kind exists too between the *Portrait of a Young Woman with a Cat* (Fig. 73) in the Berlin Museum and the *Madonna with the little St. John* (Fig. 72) in Dresden.

The Florentine Street Scene, (Fig. 80) also called *The Shelter for Travellers* is almost unique among the pictures of this time. Little scenes of daily life were often painted in the backgrounds, but only as an accompaniment of the main subject. But here, the subject of the painting is a street scene. Even if it is representing the shelter for travellers and belonged to a series depicting *The Seven Deeds of Charity*, it still remeins a purely genre painting, a procursor of little street scenes of the eighteenth century. This painting, dated ca. 1540–1550, may have been executed by Bacchiacca during a brief respite from the gloomy pomp of the Medici court. The genre elements also appears in designs for tapestries *The Month of the Year*, dated between 1543 and 1553. Yet the attribution is not convincing enough to list this work as an authentic one.

Throughout his life Bacchiacca painted several Madonnas in the manner of different artists: Perugino, Andrea del Sarto, Michelangelo and even Leonardo. He derived the composition of his *Madonna and Child* from Fra Bartolommeo's *Madonna Enthroned* in the Museo di San Marco in Florence.[25] However, he removed Madonna from her throne and placed her, together with St. Anne or St. Elisabeth and the Infant St. John, against various landscapes. This group of Madonnas includes one in Asolo, once attributed to Raphael (Pl. 14); two in Florence, in private collections (Fig. 52–53), and one in the Wildenstein Gallery in New York (Fig. 54). *The Madonna and Child with the Infant St. John* (Fig. 19), formerly attributed to Perugino, but identified as Bacchiacca by Dr. Offner in 1925, belongs despite some variations in the composition to this group.[26] Unfortunately, the present whereabouts of this lovely painting is unknown. The gentle sway of the head and neck, the virginal face, with its arched brow and faint smile, were often painted by Renaissance artists. Whereas these paintings may seem similar at first glance, one gradually begins to recognize certain distinguishing characteristics of different masters. Often too difference in coloring reveals the difference in periods—Bacchiacca's private collection, Florence Madonna (Fig. 52) is light and metallic in its tone, while the coloring of the Wildenstein painting is more intense and prominent and must be therefore of later date.

In the *Virgin and Child* (Fig. 42), formerly in the Blumenthal collection, Bacchiacca openly imitated his friend Andrea.[27] It was not possible again to trace the present location of this painting. The little panel depicting *Madonna and Child* (Fig. 20), formerly in the Countess Shuvaloff collection in St. Petersburg, is probably now in one of the Russian museums.[28] Judging from the pale photograph,

[25] *Bacchiacca and His Friends—Catalogue of an Exhibition Presented by The Baltimore Museum of Art* Jan. 10–Febr. 19, 1961. p. 22, fig. 5.
[26] R. Offner, *Bacchiacca 1494–1557, The Blessed Virgin* A Study, Jan. 1925, Fearon Galleries Publ.
[27] S. Rubinstein-Bloch, *Collection of George and Florence Blumenthal*, 1926, 1, pl. 15.
[28] V. Lazareff, "Una Madonna del Bacchiacca", *L'Arte*, 1923, 26, pp. 86–88.

this is an enchanting example of Bacchiacca's early period which shows his endeavor to attain Andrea's suave and painterly manner.

Morelli assigned the *Holy Family* (Fig. 68), formerly in the Cook collection and now in the Ambrosiana, Milan, to the late period of Bacchiacca.[29] Suida called it Bacchiacca's variation of the *Virgin of the Rocks*.[30] However, a similar composition by Perugino in the Nancy Gallery, France, rather than the famous painting by Leonardo might have been the source.[31] The general mood of the painting is leonardesque and the color-scheme—pink with yellow and blue with green—points out to the middle period.

There are excellent examples of the later Madonnas in the United States. Among the most prominent is the *Madonna* (Fig. 66) in The Baltimore Museum of Art. Its color combination is dazzling—purple-pink and green-blue, as is the treatment of draperies, which are strangely juxtaposed—i.e. whirling around the Madonna's breast or sweeping calmly from shoulders to knees. The same contrast exists between her cameo-like face, her decoratively poised hands and the chubby figure of the Infant Christ who impatiently tugs at her hair. The chiseled landscape in the distance, adapted from "Maestro Alberto Durero", the originator of many Renaissance backgrounds, is in direct contradiction to the monumental image in the foreground.

One lovely version of the same painting is the *Madonna and Child* (Fig. 67) in the collection of Mr. and Mrs. Linsky in New York. The Madonna's head is quite different from the one in Baltimore with its heavy auburn hair simply dressed and her expression of tender intimacy. Her pale face is slightly touched by the first signs of maturity. The almost screen-like rock formation in the close background is softened by flowers painted with the precision of the school of Leonardo. The leonardesque feeling prevails in the painting indicating the earlier date, possibly between thirties and forties.

The group of the Madonna and Child with the Infant St. John was a favorite composition of Bacchiacca. One of them, now in the

[29] G. Morelli, *Critical Studies of Italian Painters*, 1900, p. 109.
[30] W. Suida, *Leonardo und sein Kreis*, 1929, p. 245.
[31] W. Bombe, *Perugino*, 1914, p. 153.

26

Wildenstein Gallery in New York (Fig. 79), is based on the figure of the woman and child who can be seen in the crowd on the panel, *The Gathering of Manna* in Washington D.C. This painting of Madonna possesses all the more positive qualities of Bacchiacca; the pure and brilliant colors, the alternation of various greens and reds. On her hair, carefully looped with locks about her brow, the Madonna wears a small turban of green and rasberry red, decorated by a single jewel. The hair of both Children is fair and curly, and the little St. John wears the familiar leopard skin over his left shoulder. The coloristic treatment of the Madonna's face and hands, and the bodies of Christ and St. John are executed in the best tradition of Tuscan Mannerism. The serene group is prominent against the brown-grey wall; at the left, to complete the scene, there is a bird who drinks water which falls into a crystal cup. This painting is one of the most perfect of Bacchiacca's Madonnas. Through it one may peer into his calm and untroubled world. For the "poor" Bacchiacca, the "minor" artist, as he has been styled, lived in a time when "people moved freely in the august presence of great art, for bad art had not yet been invented"[32] despite imitation and different degrees of skill. Even in using the designs of others, the artists of the Renaissance seldom lost sight of their inherent and excellent craftmanship. This constant "give and take" united them, all great and small. In a period when art was good, so-called "minor" artists were not apt to be bad. The standard of perfection was too firmly established at an exalted level.

The paintings of Bacchiacca divided as they are into the groups of Madonnas with Christ and St. John; the biblical scenes; his Ledas and portraits demonstrate, in no small degree, his share in the interaction between the Italian Mannerists and their neighbours to the North—the Germans and Flemmings.

So much has been said about the lasting influence of Andrea del Sarto on Bacchiacca that is has become almost indisputable. But the spirit of Bacchiacca's art is so different from Andrea's that perhaps this relationship has been overemphasized. Morelly correctly noted the influence of Andrea in Bacchiacca's "manner of posing his figures, of drawing hands, of arranging draperies, and more especially in his landscape backgrounds—which, as a rule,

[32] R. A. Taylor, *Invitation to Renaissance Italy*, 1930, p. 46.

are very careful in execution".[33] The sfumato, too, in Bacchiacca's paintings is comparable to that of Andrea, but after all, this was the vocabulary of the time. Admiring and imitating Andrea, Bacchiacca remained foreign to the very soul of his art. "La bella maniera" of Andrea was either unattainable or simply alien to him. One cannot but feel that Bacchiacca had more often looked past Andrea into the bizarre world of the latter's teacher—Piero di Cosimo. Chiaroscuro, as the core of Andrea's art, did not play an important role in Bacchiacca's, and being a humble but true Mannerist, he did not try to reproduce the effect of natural light. His paintings have a clear lustre, his figures cast almost no shadows, the various parts of his paintings are equally distinct, his flowers painted with the same precision with which he painted jewels. He remained faithful to the older tradition of painting, using color instead of chiaroscuro for the modeling of the form.

Flesh tones in Bacchiacca's paintings were usually light, executed with cool greenish grey on which the contour was delicately drawn. The form was then modeled by covering the lighted spots with very pale pink, a method used by the early Italians and revived by the Mannerists. It is a typical tempera method, but Bacchiacca also used it when working with oils. Vasari mentioned oil in connection with the little studiolo for the Duke Cosimo,[34] and Borghini spoke of this medium when referring to panels for the Borgherini chamber.[35] As a pupil of Perugino, Bacchiacca was well versed in the tempera technique and probably did all his basic work with this medium. Oil was used as a finish, thus conforming to the method used by several artists of his time. These delicate glazings have often been cleaned away in former restorations leaving the underpaint and destroying the original aspect of the paintings. For color is Bacchiacca's forte clear and cool, bright and decorative, unnatural and fantastic. The primary colors—red, yellow, and blue—are highlighted with green and blue, pink and lilac in a manner similar to Byzantine and Russian icon-painters. Possibly one reason that the critics were slow in recognizing the merits of Bacchiacca's works was that their colors were often hidden under dirt and dark-

[33] G. Morelli, *Critical Studies of Italian Painters*, 1900, pp. 102–103.
[34] G. Vasari, *Vite*, VI, p. 455.
[35] R. Borghini, *Il Riposo*, Milan ed. 1807, II, p. 252.

ened varnish. Many critics disliked his coloring, finding it too naive and gay for the time when great art was mainly considered in massive forms executed in deep tones.[36]

The foliage of Bacchiacca's trees is amber green with bluish lights. Despite a cool sfumato, his figures and landscapes remain Florentine in their sharpness and graceful contour. His picturesque rocks are light grey with either a white or blue cast. His strong, precise line became bolder under the influence of the engravings of Lucas von Leyden and Dürer. The adaptation of such engravings, stylistically rooted in Quattrocento, was natural for Bacchiacca and much easier than the attempt to achieve the classic style of the High Renaissance or the Michelangelesque terribilità. He did not use these engravings because of artistic poverty. Rather, they were appropriate to the boundaries of his visual world, enriching the landscapes of his freshly colored, miniature universe. He introduced Northern houses and churches with pointed roofs, together with vignettes of peasant life in the backgrounds, lending a Germanic quality to many paintings. The repeated use of one and the same motif in different paintings, give his art both a monotonous and a harmonious quality, analogous to the ritournelle of a folk-song.

Of all Bacchiacca's works, his decorative paintings and designs for the ducal court are the least known. Vasari had listed them briefly and without comment.[37] Not much is left of the decoration of the ceiling in the terrace of the Palazzo Vecchio, but geometrical designs, medallions with the heads of the bearded warriors and women, flowers and fruit, and the only known signature of Bacchiacca is to be found there. It is written on the golden ball adorning the bridle of one of the horses—Franc. Bach. Fac.[38] None of his presently identified paintings bears this signature or a variation thereof. Perhaps it was included there as a spontaneous whim of the artist. The notation of the signature, remote from the eyes of spectators, again emphasies his modesty. Bacchiacca was over fifty when he worked on these decorations in 1552–1553. He had achieved a considerable degree of artistic perfection and enjoyed a

[36] O. Spengler, *Untergang des Abendlandes*, 1918, p. 81.
[37] G. Vasari, *Vite*, VI, pp. 455–456.
[38] A. Lensi, *Palazzo Vecchio*, 1929, p. 128.

certain measure of success. There was no attempt on his parts to soar to great heights and to grasp the unattainable.

Bacchiacca's designs for the tapestries the *Months*, with little scenes of rural life, show again the peaceful and familiar world into which he retreated, from time to time, as if tired by more monumental works. The tapestries were woven by the Flemish master, Johannes Rost. In place of his own signature he wove a big piece of roast beef, a bit of jovial Flemish realism well suited to the scenes of Bacchiacca.[39]

Another series of the tapestries, *Groteschi* present the lively juxtapositions of animals, birds fish, fruits, and fantastic profiles, woven on a sunny yellow background. Two tapestries of this series are now in the Palazzo Davanzati in Florence.[40]

Bacchiacca was a good draughtsman, but his drawings have had the same strange fate as his paintings. Attributed to great artists, they are praised; given to Bacchiacca, they are the poor imitation of the great. Little landscape drawings with rivers, trees, and castles are lively and expressive. Sometimes he drew the view of Mugello— his birth place—and oddly wrote its name right in the center of the drawing. The controversial *Woman with folded Arms* in the Uffizi, formerly attributed to Leonardo, was assigned to Bacchiacca by Morelli and to Pontormo by Berenson.[41] There is a portrait executed after this drawing, attributed to Pontormo and copied by Degas during his stay in Italy. The drawing of a woman, seated in profile, reproduced by Paula Barocchi in her "Il Rosso Fiorentino", together with five other drawings by Bacchiacca, has almost an eighteenth century French quality.[42] Most of the references to his drawings are scattered in books on other artists: in Clapp's "Jacopo Carucci da Pontormo";[43] in works on Michelangelo by Thode,[44] de Tolnay[45] and Goldscheider;[46] in Berenson's "Drawings of the

[39] M. Tinti, "Il Bacchiacca e i suoi Arazzi", *Dedaio*, 1920, I, pp. 803–817.
[40] L. Berti, Palazzo Davanzati, 1958, p. 15.
[41] G. Morelli, *Critical Studies of Italian Painters*, 1900, p. 113.
[42] P. Barocchi, *Il Rosso Fiorentino*, 1950, Pl. 200.
[43] F. M. Clapp, *Jacopo Carucci da Pontormo*, 1916, pp. 78, 95, 129, 231.
[44] H. Thode, *Michelangelo und das Ende der Renaissance*, Vol. 3, p. 496.
[45] C. de Tolnay, *The Youth of Michelangelo*, 1947, Vol. 5, *The Final Period*, Nos. 111, 113, 114.
[46] L. Goldscheider, ed. *Michelangelo's Drawings*, pp. 41–42.

Florentine Painters".[47] Charles Loeser attributed to Bacchiacca the drawings "Marchesa di Pescara" and "Count Canossa".[48] Luisa Marcucci reproduced eighteen drawings by him in her "Contributo al Bachiaca".[49] There was no attempt made to catalogue them.

Consisting of many borrowings, Bacchiacca's compositions are nevertheless a delight, even graceful in their awkwardness. They reflect an inner lack of complexity and conflict, a harmony with the external world which even the tension of the Florentine Mannerism could not destroy. He was a Mannerist from the beginning; as a mature artist, his paintings became more sophisticated and sad in expression, more refined and coquittish in their attitudes, but never did they lose their emotional balance.

Since new paintings are constantly being discovered, the number of Bacchiacca's works is steadily growing. Among the Andrea del Sartos and Albertinellis dispersed in European collections some lovely Bacchiaccas may still wait to be discovered. The repetition of the same theme is more explainable when one remembers that he painted works which were sent to France and England.[50] But even what is known now, reveals an interesting artist. Morelli might well have been pleased with the growing appreciation of the forgotten artist to whom he dedicated a few pages in his "Critical Studies of Italian Painters" in 1900. The image of a little bird drinking fresh water from a crystal cup in the *Madonna* (Fig. 79) in the Wildenstein Gallery is a very incarnation of the art of Francesco Ubertini called il Bacchiacca. He peacefully imbibed the purity of art, confined for him in one cup, so transparent indeed that all the deceptive qualities were readily visible. The "grand manner" is absent from his art, as also from his life, and he is content among the pilfered treasures which he transformed into his own works, by means of his gift for color and composition and his enchanting way of dismissing problems.

[47] B. Berenson, *Drawings of the Florentine Painters*, 1903, Vol. 1, pp. 300–302; Vol. 2, p. 11.

[48] C. Loeser, *Disegni Italiani della Raccolta Malcolm*, Archivio Storico dell'Arte, 1897, p. 352, Nos. 55, 56.

[49] L. Marcucci, *Contributo al Bachiaca*, Bolletino d'Arte, 1958, pp. 26–39.

[50] G. Vasari, *Vite*, VI, p. 455.

CATALOGUE RAISONNÉ OF THE AUTHENTIC PAINTINGS BY BACCHIACCA

RESURRECTION   Fig. 1.
Dijon Museum, France

PANEL: Very small size.

DATE: about 1510–1515.

DESCRIPTION: The composition is derived from the *Resurrection* by Perugino in the Vatican Gallery and the predella panel of the same subject
attributed to Perugino in the Metropolitan Museum, New York. The
background shows the difference between the Florentine and the Umbrian treatment of the landscape.

BIBLIOGRAPHY: U. Gnoli, "L'Arte italiana in alcune gallerie francesi di
provincia", *Rassegna d'Arte*, 1908, pp. 186–189.   G. Frizzoni, "Interno
a due dipinti die scuole italiane nel Museo di Digione", *Rassegna d'Arte*,
1906, pp. 186–189.   A. McComb, "Bacchiacca", *The Art Bulletin*, VIII,
1926, pp. 152–153.

NOLI ME TANGERE   Fig. 2.
Christ Church, Oxford.

PANEL: $16\frac{1}{4} \times 13\frac{1}{4}$ inches.

DATE: ca 1505–1518.

DESCRIPTION: An early peruginescue work. Attributed to Bacchiacca by
Morelli.

BIBLIOGRAPHY: G. Morelli, *Critical Studies of Italian Painters*, 1900, pt. 1,
p. 101.   T. Borenius, *Catalogue of the Pictures in Christ Church, Oxford*,
1916, p. 36.   A. McComb, "Bacchiacca", *The Art Bulletin*, VIII, 1926,
p. 165.

PREACHING OF CHRIST   Fig. 3.
Christ Church, Oxford

PANEL: $35\frac{1}{4} \times 23\frac{3}{4}$ inches.

DATE: ca 1505–1518.

DESCRIPTION: An early Umbrian composition with a peruginesque building in the center. Also erroneously called THE RAISING OF LAZA-
RUS.

BIBLIOGRAPHY: G. Morelli, *Critical Studies of Italian Painters*, 1900, pt. 1,
p. 101.   T. Borenius, *Catalogue of the Pictures in Christ Church, Oxford*,
1916, p. 36.   A. McComb, "Bacchiacca", *The Art Bulletin*, VIII, 1926,
p. 165.

DESCENT FROM THE CROSS (Deposition)   Fig. 4.
Museo Civico, Bassano Veneto

PANEL: c. 24 × 20 inches

DATE: ca. 1515.

DESCRIPTION: An early work based on the composition of Perugino. Also attributed to the School of Perugino.

BIBLIOGRAPHY: O. Fischel, *Die Zeichnungen der Umbrer*, 1917, p. 61, fig. 69a.   A. McComb, "Bacchiacca", *The Art Bulletin*, VIII, 1926, p. 149. U. Middeldorf, "Sull'attività della bottega di Jacopo Sansovino", *Rivista d'Arte*, 8, 1936, pp. 252–253, 259–60.   L. Magagnato, "Il Museo Civico di Bassano del Grappa", *Emporium*, XVIII, 1953, p. 26.   S. J. Freedberg, *Painting of the High Renaissance in Rome and Florence*, 1961, p. 501, Pl. 627.

HOLY FAMILY   Fig. 5.
Staatsgalerie Stuttgart

PANEL: 24½ × 19¾ inches.

DATE: 1520–1530.

DESCRIPTION: Like the *Madonna and Child* once in the Blumenthal collection, this painting is derived from Andrea del Sarto's composition of the Holy Family in the Wallace Collection, London and in the Barberini Palace, Rome. Acquired by the museum in 1857 from an art dealer in Stuttgart.

BIBLIOGRAPHY: S. J. Freedberg, *Andrea del Sarto, Catalogue Raisonné*, 1963, p. 183.

CHRIST CARRYING THE CROSS   Fig. 6.
Collection of Mr. John Drury-Lowe, England.

PANEL: 18 × 21½ inches.

DATE: about 1520.

DESCRIPTION: A combination of peruginesque drawing and Bacchiacca's coloring. The attribution to Bacchiacca was made by Dr. Richter. Salvini listed it among the false attributions in the Thieme-Becker Lexicon. A replica of this picture was at Brompton Oratorium, London.
BIBLIOGRAPHY: J. P. Richter, *Catalogue of Pictures at Loko Park*, 1901, p. 17.   A. Cameron Taylor, "On Christ carrying the Cross", *The Connoisseur*, 1903, p. 89.   B. Berenson, *The Florentine Painters*, 1909, p. 109   R. Salvini, "Francesco Ubertini", *Thieme-Becker*, XXXIII, 1939, pp. 522–523.   Works of Art from Midland Houses, *Catalogue of the Exhibition July 18–Sept. 6, 1953*. p. 30.

36

ADAM AND EVE WITH THEIR CHILDREN   Fig. 7
John G. Johnson Collection, Museum of Fine Arts, Philadelphia.

PANEL: $13\frac{7}{8}$ × 11 inches.

DATE: c. 1518; c. 1516 (Freedberg).

DESCRIPTION: The composition is based on the cartoon of Perugino *Apollo and Marsyas*. The background is derived from the engraving of Dürer *Adam and Eve*. Formerly Frizzoni, Milan.

BIBLIOGRAPHY: G. Morelli, *Critical Studies of Italian Painters*, 1900, pt. 1, p. 101.   B. Berenson, *The Florentine Painters of the Renaissance*, 1907, pp. 102–103.   B. Berenson, *Catalogue of the J. G. Johnson collection* 1913, I, p. 281.   A. Venturi, *Storia dell'Arte Italiana*, 1925, IX, p. 475. A. McComb, "Bacchiacca", *The Art Bulletin*, VIII, 1926, p. 161. A. Scharf, "Bacchiacca: A New Contribution", *The Burlington Magazine*, LXX, 1937, p. 65.   L. Burroughs, "A Painting by Bacchiacca", *Bulletin of the Metropolitan Museum of Art*, XXXIV, 1939, p. 98.   H. B. Wehle, *A Catalogue of Italian, Spanish and Byzantine Paintings*, The Metropolitan *Museum of Art*, 1940, p. 67.   L. Marcucci, "Contributo al Bachiaca", *Bolletino d'Arte*, XLIII, 1958, p. 32.   S. J. Freedberg, *Painting of the High Renaissance in Rome and Florence*, 1961, p. 502, Pl. 628.

STORY FROM THE LIFE OF JOSEPH   Fig. 8.
The National Gallery, London.

PANEL: $11\frac{1}{4}$ × 3 inches.

DATE: 1515–1516.

DESCRIPTION: Cat. No. 1218 shows two scenes: the envoy of Joseph conducting the young Benjamin, at the left and at the right, Benjamin and his brothers at the feet of Joseph. There are drawings in the Louvre, in the Uffizi and in the Albertina which served as cartoons for this picturee. Bacchiacca used several figures again in other compositions. Both panels belong to the series executed for the Borgherini family in Florence. Formerly Nerli, Italy; Rev. J. Sanford, England.

BIBLIOGRAPHY: G. Vasari, ed. Milanesi, 1878/82, V, p. 343.   A. v. Reumont, *Andrea del Sarto*, Leipzig, 1835, pp. 133, 137, 138.   B. Berenson, *Drawings of the Florentine Painters*, 1903, nos. 186, 187, 189.   A. McComb, "Bacchiacca", *The Art Bulletin*, VIII, 1926, p. 157.   B. Nicolson, "The Sanford Collection", *The Burlington Magazine*, 1955, pp. 207–213.   S. J. Freedberg, *Painting of the High Renaissance in Rome and Florence*, 1961, Pls. 629, 631.

STORY FROM THE LIFE OF JOSEPH   Fig. 9.
National Gallery, London.

PANEL: 11¼ × 3 inches.

DATE: 1515–1516.

DESCRIPTION: Cat. No. 1219 shows the return of the brothers with gifts, and the little Benjamin; their reception by Joseph and their departure. Formerly Nerli, Italy; Rev. J. Sanford, England.

BIBLIOGRAPHY: (same as above).

STORY FROM THE LIFE OF JOSEPH   Fig. 10.
Borghese Gallery, Rome. (Cat. No. 425).

TRANSFERRED FROM PANEL TO CANVAS: 10¼ × 7½ inches.

DATE: 1515–1516.

DESCRIPTION: Scene of the arrest of Joseph's brothers. The figures of soldiers, in the foreground, were later used in the *Baptism*, formerly in the Mond collection, and in *The Persecution of St. Barbara*, formerly in the collection Böhler, Munich.

BIBLIOGRAPHY: G. Vasari, *Vite*, V, p. 343.   J. Manilli, *Villa Borghese fuori di Porta Pinciana, Roma*, 1650, pp. 111–112.   A. McComb, "Bacchiacca", *The Art Bulletin*, VIII, 1926, p. 157.   A. Pigler, *Barockthemen*. 1956, pt. 1, pp. 60, 86.   L. Ferrara, *Galleria Borghese*, 1956, p. 38. P. della Pergola, *Catalogo di Galleria Borghese*, 1959, II, Dipinti. Pls. 8–12. S. J. Freedberg, *Painting of the High Renaissance in Rome and Florence*, 1961, Pls. 630, 632.

STORY FROM THE LIFE OF JOSEPH   Fig. 11.
Borghese Gallery, Rome, (Cat. No. 427)

PANEL: 10¼ × 7½ inches.

DATE: 1515–1516.

DESCRIPTION: Joseph sold to the Ismaelites.

BIBLIOGRAPHY: (same as above).

STORY FROM THE LIFE OF JOSEPH   Fig. 12.
Borghese Gallery, Rome, (Cat. No. 440).

PANEL: 10¼ × 7½ inches.

DATE: 1515–1516.

DESCRIPTION: The discovery of Joseph's cup in Benjamin's sack.

BIBLIOGRAPHY: (same as above).

STORY FROM THE LIFE OF JOSEPH   Fig. 13.
Borghese Gallery, Rome, (Cat. No. 442).

PANEL: $10\frac{1}{4} \times 7\frac{1}{2}$ inches.

DATE: 1515–1516.

DESCRIPTION: The searching of the sacks of Joseph's brothers. In the background, at the right, a view of a Northern house and a church with a pointed roof.

BIBLIOGRAPHY: (same as above).

MADONNA WITH ST. ELISABETH AND THE   Fig. 14.
INFANT ST. JOHN
Canonica della Parrochia, Asolo.

PANEL: 28×21 inches.

DATE: about 1520.

DESCRIPTION: The earliest version of a composition later repeated three times with slightly altered details and differences in coloring. This picture was formerly attributed to Raphael. Morelli attributed it to Bacchiacca. Berenson and Poggi accepted his attribution. Formerly Bertoldi, Italy.

BIBLIOGRAPHY: B. Bertoldi, publ. *Di una nuova tavoletta di Raffaele*, Asolo, 1897.   F. de Amicis, *Raffaele Sanzio da Urbino e la sua Madonna delle Missione che si conserva in Asolo Veneto nella Raccolta Bertoldi*, Genova, 1906. G. Poggi, "Di una Madonna di Bacchiacca attribuito a Raffaelo", *Monatshefte*, 1908, pp. 275–280.   A. McComb, "Bacchiacca", *The Art Bulletin*, VIII, 1926, p. 149.

TOBIAS AND THE ANGEL   Fig. 15.
Uffizi, Florence.

PANEL: $12\frac{1}{8} \times 9\frac{3}{4}$ inches.

DATE: about 1520.

DESCRIPTION: Poggi pointed out that the head of the Angel is very similar to that of the Madonna in the Asolo picture. (Fig. 14). The treatment of trees and sky is also identical in the two paintings.

BIBLIOGRAPHY: C. Gamba, "Quadri nuovamente esposti agli Uffizi", *Bolletino d'Arte*, 1907, pt. 1, pp. 20–22.   G. Poggi, "Di una Madonna di Bacchiacca attribuito a Raffaelo", *Monatshefte*, 1908, pp. 275–280. A. McComb, "Bacchiacca", *The Art Bulletin*, VIII, 1926, p. 153.

CREATION OF EVE   Fig. 16.
Present Whereabouts unknown.

PANEL: 26 × 20½ inches.

DATE: 1518–1520.

DESCRIPTION: A variation of the composition by Fra Bartolommeo in the
Seattle Museum. The landscape is different and shows the influence of
Northern engravings. The figure of God was later used for that of Moses
in *The Gathering of Manna* in the National Gallery, Washington D.C.
There is a drawing of the same composition in the Private Collection in
Sweden which has been attributed to Raphael but which could be more
probably ascribed to Bacchiacca. Formerly Neues Palais, Potsdam.

BIBLIOGRAPHY: A. Scharf, "Bacchiacca: A New Contribution", *The
Burlington Magazine*, Febr. 1937, pp. 60–70.   G. Fiocco, "Fra Barto-
lommeo e Raffaello", *Rivista d'Arte*, 1954, XXIX, pp. 43–53.   S. J.
Freedberg, *Painting of the High Renaissance in Rome and Florence*, 1961,
Pl. 634 (Drawing in Stockholm).

GHISMONDA WITH THE HEART OF GUISCARDO   Fig. 17.
S. H. Kress Foundation, U.S.A.

PANEL: diam. 26⅝ inches.

DATE: c. 1520–1521.

DESCRIPTION: This tondo, formerly called *The Crystal-Gazing Scene*, shows
an illustration of the story told by Fiametta in *Decameron* of Boccaccio.
The coloring is intense; the landscape in the distant background still
Peruginesque. The reverse of the picture bears the conjoined arms of the
Carducci and Giudetti families. Formerly White, London.

BIBLIOGRAPHY: B. Berenson, *The Florentine Painters of the Renaissance*, 1907,
pp. 102–103.   T. Borenius, "Allegory", *The Burlington Magazine*, Vol.
XL, 1922, pp. 131–132.   A. Venturi, *Storia dell'Arte Italiana*, IX, 1925,
p. 475.   *Preliminary Catalogue of Paintings and Sculpture*, National Gallery
of Art, Washington, D.C., 1941, p. 10.   *Book of illustrations*, ibid., p. 58,
Cat. No. 272.   *The Samuel H. Kress Collection*, A Catalog of European
Paintings and Sculpture, 1961, pp. 50–53.

PREACHING OF ST. JOHN THE BAPTIST   Fig. 18.
Museum of Fine Arts, Budapest.

PANEL: 28 × 36⅝ inches.

DATE: c. 1520.

DESCRIPTION: Morelli attributed this painting to Bacchiacca's third and last period. It is, however, still a mixture of Umbrian and Florentine characteristics and shows no trace of Michelangelo's influence. According to Dr. Pigler this painting had been repainted several times which produced a great change in certain details. St. John has a brown hair garment and a crimson mantle; his listeners are dressed in bright colors—brilliant blue, orange yellow and deep cinnober red. Formerly Bacciocchi, Florence.

BIBLIOGRAPHY: G. Morelli, *The Borghese and Doria-Pamphili Galleries*, 1900, p. 101 f.   B. Berenson, *Florentine Painters of the Renaissance*, 1907, pp. 102–103.   A. Venturi, *Storia dell'Arte Italiana*, 1925, IX, pt. 1, p. 474. A. McComb, "Bacchiacca", *The Art Bulletin*, VIII, 1926, p. 150. Dr. Andreas Pigler, *A Letter dated May 7*, 1960.

VIRGIN AND CHILD WITH THE INFANT ST. JOHN   Fig. 19.
Present whereabouts unknown.

CANVAS: 43 × 33½ inches.

DATE: c. 1520.

DESCRIPTION: This beautiful picture was formerly attributed to Perugino. Dr. R. Offner identified it as Bacchiacca in 1925. The background landscape at the left with an arched bridge shows an affinity with that of the copy of *Leda with the Swan* of Leonardo in the Borghese Gallery. Formerly Fearon Galleries, New York.

BIBLIOGRAPHY: R. Offner, *Bacchiacca 1494–1557.   The Blessed Virgin, Christ, and the Infant St. John, A Study.*, 1925, Fearon Galleries publ. A. McComb, "Bacchiacca", *The Art Bulletin*, VIII, 1926, p. 158–161.

MADONNA AND CHILD   Fig. 20.
Hermitage, Leningrad.?

PANEL: 12 × 9¾ inches.

DATE: c. 1520.

DESCRIPTION: According to Lazareff this is one of the best pictures of Bacchiacca's early period. The composition is peruginesque; the Child is adopted from Andrea del Sarto. The Madonna wears a red dress, a blue-green mantle and a rose turban. The wooden bench and the parapet are grey. Not listed in the Hermitage Catalogue of 1958. Formerly Countess Shuvaloff, St. Petersburg.

BIBLIOGRAPHY: V. Lazareff, "Una Madonna del Bacchiacca", *L'Arte*, 1923, pp. 86–88.

SCENES FROM THE LIFE OF ST. ACASIO (predella)   Fig. 21.
BAPTISM OF ST. ACASIO AND HIS COMPANIONS
Uffizi, Florence.

PANEL: $9\frac{1}{4}$ × 11 inches.

DATE: 1521.

DESCRIPTION: This predella consisting of three scenes from the Life of St. Acasio was painted for an altarpiece *Storia de' Martiri* by Giovanni Antonio Sogliani in San Lorenzo. It has been transferred to Uffizi in 1866. For the scene of the baptism of the Saint and his companions, Bacchiacca used the engraving by Lucas von Leyden *Baptism of Christ*. The colors are light and smooth.

BIBLIOGRAPHY: G. Vasari, *Vite*, VI, p. 455.   A. Cocchi, *Le Chiese di Firenze*, 1903, p. 34.   M. Cruttwell, *Florentine Galleries*, pt. 1, 1907, p. 125.   A. Scharf, "Bacchiacca: A New Contribution", *The Burlington Magazine*, 1937, pp. 60–70.   A. McComb, "Bacchiacca", *The Art Bulletin*, VIII, 1926, p. 153–154.   H. S. Merritt, *Bacchiacca Studies; The Use of Imitation*, Princeton, 1958.   S. J. Freedberg, *Painting of the High Renaissance in Rome and Florence*, 1961, Pls. 636–637.

SCENES FROM THE LIFE OF ST. ACASIO   Fig. 22.
MARTYRDOM OF ST. ACASIO AND HIS COMPANIONS
Uffizi, Florence.

PANEL: $9\frac{1}{4}$ × 11 inches.

DATE: 1521.

DESCRIPTION: The composition is based mainly on the borrowings from the engravings by Lucas von Leyden.

BIBLIOGRAPHY: (same as above).

SCENES FROM THE LIFE OF ST. ACASIO   Fig. 23.
ST. ACASIO DEFEATING THE REBELS
WITH THE HELP OF ANGELS
Uffizi, Florence.

PANEL: $9\frac{1}{4}$ × 11 inches.

DATE: 1521.

DESCRIPTION: A battle scene showing the influence of the cartoons by Leonardo and Michelangelo.

BIBLIOGRAPHY: (same as above).

THE PERSECUTION OF ST. BARBARA

Fig. 24.

Present whereabouts unknown.

PANEL: 16¾ × 14 inches.

DATE: 1520–1530.

DESCRIPTION: The landscape is painted in cool bluish tones. The figure of the warrior and his white horse are very close to that in the predella scene of St. Acasio in the Uffizi. The figures of a soldier and a cloaked man behind him, at the left, are repeated from *Joseph's Brethern arrested* in the Borghese Gallery. Formerly Böhler, Swarzenski, Germany.

BIBLIOGRAPHY: B. Berenson, *Italian Pictures of the Renaissance*, 1932, pp. 34–35.   A. Scharf, "Bacchiacca: A New Contribution", *The Burlington Magazine*, 1937, pp. 60–70.   A Letter from Mr. J. Böhler, dated March 3rd, 1960.

CARITAS

Fig. 25.

The Metropolitan Museum of Art, New York.

PANEL: 15¾ × 9¼ inches.

DATE: 1520–1525.

DESCRIPTION: The figure of Caritas is the same as that of Eve with her children in the painting in the Johnson collection, Philadelphia. The background is different and the coloring much lighter and smoother. Formerly Hope, Edinburgh; Locker-Lampson, London.

BIBLIOGRAPHY: R. Langton-Douglas, *Italian pictures collected by Godfrey Locker-Lampson*, n. d., No. 11, ill., p. 10.   A. Scharf, "Bacchiacca: A New Contribution", *The Burlington Magazine*, Febr. 1937, pp. 60–70. L. Burroughs, "A Painting by Bacchiacca", *Bulletin of the Metropolitan Museum of Art*, XXXIV, 1939, pp. 97–98.   H. B. Wehle, *A Catalogue of Italian, Spanish and Byzantine Paintings*, The Metropolitan Museum of Art, 1940, pp. 67–68.   J. Allen & E. Gardner, *A Concise Catalogue of the European Paintings in The Metropolitan Museum of Art*, 1954, p. 7.

ST. JOHN THE BAPTIST IN THE WILDERNESS

Fig. 26.

BOB JONES University Art Gallery, Greenville, S. C.

PANEL: 14 × 9½ inches.

DATE: 1521–1523.

DESCRIPTION: Dr. E. Thietze-Conrat suggests that this is a part of the decoration of the Borgherini Chamber. The landscape, however, is already very typical of Bacchiacca. The pose of the Saint is derived from the composition *The Creation of Eve* based on the painting by Fra Bartolommeo, and, probably executed about the same time. The coloring

43

of the body is warm and pink; the golden-brown tone prevails in the foliage, the hair of St. John and the skin of the deers.

BIBLIOGRAPHY: *Exhibition of European and American Masters*, High Museum of Art, Atlanta, 1949, Cat. No. 8.   E. Tietze-Conrat, *The BOB JONES University Collection of Religious Paintings*, 1954, p. 52.

ST. JOHN THE BAPTIST IN THE WILDERNESS   Fig. 27.
The Newhouse Galleries, New York.

PANEL: $16\frac{1}{2}$ × $11\frac{3}{8}$ inches.

DATE: 1523–1525.

DESCRIPTION: A slightly changed version of the composition in the BOB JONES University.

BIBLIOGRAPHY: *Bacchiacca and His Friends*, An Exhibition Presented by The Baltimore Museum of Art, Jan. 10–Febr. 19, 1961. p. 36.

LEGEND OF THE DEAD KING   Fig. 28.
Gemäldegalerie, Dresden, Germany.

PANEL: $33\frac{1}{2}$ × $77\frac{1}{4}$ inches.

DATE: 1523.

DESCRIPTION: Probably a side of a long cassone painted for the chamber in the Benintendi house in Florence. The subject and composition are unusual. The architectural setting is a blend of peruginesque and Florentine compositions. The house in the background, at the extreme left, is taken from Lukas von Leyden's engraving and is used in many of Bacchiacca's paintings.

BIBLIOGRAPHY: G. Vasari, *Vite*, VI, p. 455.   A. McComb, "Bacchiacca", *The Art Bulletin*, 1926, VIII, p. 153.   W. Stechov, "Shooting at Father's Corpse", *The Art Bulletin*, 1942, 24, pp. 213–225.   H. S. Merritt, *Bacchiacca Studies; The Use of Imitation*, Princeton, 1958.   S. J. Freedberg, *Painting of the High Renaissance in Rome and Florence*, 1961, P. 638.

BAPTISM OF CHRIST   Fig. 29.
Staatliche Museen, Berlin.

PANEL: $29\frac{1}{2}$ × $65\frac{3}{8}$ inches.

DATE: 1523–1525.

DESCRIPTION: This picture was painted for the decoration of a chamber in the House of Benintendi. It might have been a side of a cassone or a part of a piece of furniture. This long panel demonstrates Bacchiacca's method of using the same figures in different compositions.

44

BIBLIOGRAPHY: G. Vasari, *Vite*, VI, pp. 455. G. Poggi, "Di una Madonna di Bacchiacca attribuito a Raffaelo", *Monatshefte*, 1908, pp. 275–280. A. McComb, "Bacchiacca", *The Art Bulletin*, 1926, VIII, pp. 149–50.

LAST SUPPER   Fig. 30.
Brooks Memorial Art Gallery, Memphis, Tennessy.

PANEL: $31\frac{1}{4}$ × 58 inches.

DATE: c. 1523–1525.

DESCRIPTION: The composition is based on the engraving by Marcantonio Raimondi. The landscape, seen through the window in the central wall, shows the Agony in the Garden. The walls are greenish grey; the garments of the Apostles of bright colors. The treatment of dresses and mantles shows the characteristic V-folds mentioned by Morelli. The little white dog, gnawing a bone under the table, appears in several paintings by Bacchiacca. Formerly Sir Herbert Cook, Richmond, England.

BIBLIOGRAPHY: T. Borenius, *Catalogue of the Collection of Sir Herbert Cook at Daughty House in Richmond*, 1913, No. 41. A. McComb, "Bacchiacca", *The Art Bulletin*, VIII, 1926, p. 165.

THE VISION OF ST. BERNARD   Fig. 31.
Palazzo Venezia, Rome.

PANEL: $14\frac{1}{2}$ × $17\frac{1}{3}$ inches.

DATE: 1520–1529.

DESCRIPTION: A small painting bright in color. The figure of the Saint is similar to that of *St. Francis Receiving the Stigmata* in the collection of Viscount Lee of Foreham, London. The vision of the Madonna in the sky is a variation of the composition used later for the *Madonna and Child* in the Baltimore Museum and in the Linsky collection. The nude figure of the devil in the background at the left appears again in the *Martyrs of Ararat* and is derived from the famous statue of "Laocoon". Formerly Sterbini, Rome.

BIBLIOGRAPHY: A. Venturi, *La Galleria Sterbini a Roma*, 1906, p. 133, fig. 56. A. Venturi, *Storia dell'Arte Italiana*, 1925, IX, pt. 1, p. 474. A. Santangelo, *Museo di Palazzo Venezia*, 1948, p. 17.

ST. FRANCIS RECEIVING THE STIGMATA   Fig. 32.
Collection of Viscount Lee of Fareham, London.

PANEL: $12\frac{1}{2}$ × $15\frac{3}{4}$ inches.

DATE: ca. 1520–1529.

DESCRIPTION: It is possible that this panel belongs to a series of paintings depicting the Lives of Saints. St. Francis wearing a grey habit kneels in the center of the painting. At the left, Brother Leo is witnessing the miracle. The landscape shows the familiar grey rocks and bushes and the Northern church.

BIBLIOGRAPHY: T. Borenius, *Catalogue of the Collection of Lee of Foreham, London, at 18 Kensington Palace*, II, Pl. No. 88.   R. Langton-Douglas, *Album 1st of Viscount Lee of Foreham Collection*, Cat. 26, 2 (88).

TOBIAS AND THE ANGEL   Fig. 33.
Wadsworth Atheneum, Hartford, Connecticut.

PANEL: $15\frac{3}{4} \times 12\frac{7}{8}$ inches.

DATE: 1520–1525.

DESCRIPTION: Tobias wears a pale blue garment. The Angel is dressed in pink and yellow with a touch of pale gold about the hem of his tunic. His wings are blue and yellow-brown. The white dog, borrowed from the engraving by Lucas von Leyden *The Prodigal Son*, smells at the fish in the foreground. The landscape is greenish blue. Formerly Rieffel-Müller, Frankfurt am Main.

BIBLIOGRAPHY: B. Berenson, *Italian Pictures of the Renaissance*, 1932, p. 35. *Alte Meister aus Frankfurter Privatbesitz*, Staedel Institut, Frankfurt a.M. 1925, No. 5, ill.   A. McComb, "Bacchiacca", *The Art Bulletin*, VIII, 1926, p. 167.   F. Lugt, "Man and Angel", *Gazette des Beaux-Arts*, 1944, p. 326, note 8.   Gazzanti, ed., *Enciclopedia della Pittura Italiana*, 1950, (A-G).

TOBIAS AND THE ANGEL   Fig. 34.
Present whereabouts unknown.

PANEL: $15\frac{3}{4} \times 13\frac{7}{8}$ inches.

DATE: c. 1523–1525.

DESCRIPTION: A version of the picture in the Wadsworth Atheneum. The landscape has all the familiar details: the group of trees, grey rocks, white house, at the left, and small figures at the right. The white dog lies on the ground in the center foreground in the same pose as in the painting *Last Supper* in the Brooks Memorial Art Gallery, Memphis. Formerly Simon, Berlin; Trotti, Paris.

BIBLIOGRAPHY: *Archiv für Kunstgeschichte*, 1914, 2, Taf. 117.   A. Venturi, *Storia dell'Arte Italiana*, 1925, IX, pt. 1, p. 464.

DESCENT FROM THE CROSS
Uffizi, Florence.

Fig. 35.

PANEL: c. 24 × 20 inches

DATE: c. 1518.

DESCRIPTION: A variation of the Deposition in Bassano with a landscape typical of Bacchiacca. Painted for the Convent of S. Frediano in Florence, later taken to S. Maria Maddalena de'Pazzi. Transferred to Uffizi in 1867.

BIBLIOGRAPHY: G. Vasari, *Vite*, VI, p. 455.   O. Fischel, *Die Zeichnungen der Umbrer*, 1917, p. 69.   M. Cruttwell, *Florentine Galleries*, 1907, 1 pt., p. 125.   A. McComb, "Bacchiacca", *The Art Bulletin*, VIII, p. 162. U. Middeldorf, "Sull'attivita del bottega di Jacopo Sansovino", *Rivista d'Arte*, 1936, 8, p. 252.   S. J. Freedberg, *Painting of the High Renaissance in Rome and Florence*, 1961, Pl. 633.

BAPTISM OF CHRIST
Vassar College, Poughkeepsie, N.Y.

Fig. 36.

CANVAS (TRANSFERRED FROM THE PANEL): 38½ × 31 inches.

DATE: 1523–1525.

DESCRIPTION: A variation of the *Baptism* painted for Benintendi Palace with reduced number of figures and slightly changed landscape. Very bright coloring. Formerly Sanders, London; Pratt, U.S.A.

BIBLIOGRAPHY: O. S. Tonks, *Mr. Charles M. Pratt's Gift to Vassar College*, Sribners, 1918, p. 767.   A. Venturi, *Storia dell'Arte Italiana*, 1925, IX, pt. 1, pp. 460–462.   A. McComb, "Bacchiacca", *The Art Bulletin*, 1926, VIII, p. 158.   L. Marcucci, "Contributo al Bacchiaca", *Bolletino d'Arte*, 1958, XLIII, p. 32.

BAPTISM OF CHRIST
Present Whereabouts unknown.

Fig. 37.

PANEL: 23 × 16½ inches.

DATE: 1520–1525.

DESCRIPTION: The group of Christ and St. John the Baptist is taken from the Perugino's composition of which several variations are in existance. St. John wears a brown spotted fur and a rose mantle lined with crimson. The seated man at the right foreground is repeated from the scene of *Baptism* in the predella of St. Acasio. The group at the left is taken from the *Scenes from the Life of Joseph* in the Borghese Gallery. The complete description of colors is given in the Catalogue of the Mond Collection by Richter. Formerly Mond, London, Costa, Italy.

47

BIBLIOGRAPHY: J. P. Richter, *The Mond Collection*, London, 1910, pl. 18. G. Frizzoni, "La Raccolta Mond ed opere attinenti alla medesima", *Rassegna d'Arte*, 1910, XI, p. 46.   H. S. Merritt, *Bacchiacca Studies; The Use of Imitation*, Princeton, 1958.

BAPTISM OF CHRIST   *(not illustrated)*   Fig. 38.
Palazzo Venezia, Rome.

PANEL: small

DATE: c. 1520–1525.

DESCRIPTION: A small panel with the blend of peruginesque figures and the Florentine landscape. Not mentioned in the catalogue of the Palazzo Venezia of 1948. Formerly Hertz, Rome.

BIBLIOGRAPHY: G. Frizzoni, "Intorno a due dipinti di scuole italiane", *Rassegna d'Arte*, 1906, pp. 186–189.   R. Salvini, "Francesco Ubertini", *Thieme-Becker Lexicon*, XXXIII, pp. 522–23.

PORTRAIT OF A YOUNG LUTE PLAYER   Fig. 39.
The Isaac Delgado Museum, New Orleans.

PANEL: 38⅔ × 28⅔ inches.

DATE: 1522–1525.

DESCRIPTION: The young man, seated on a parapet, wears a purple pink garment with green-blue sleeves. At the left in the background is a Triumph of Love borrowed from an anonymous engraving of the 15th century. Formerly Barker, London; Butler, London; Beit, England.

BIBLIOGRAPHY: B. Berenson, *The Florentine Painters of the Renaissance*, 1907, pp. 102–103.   W. v. Bode, *Catalogue of the Otto Beit Collection* 1913. A. Venturi, *Storia dell'Arte Italiana*, 1925, IX, pt. 1, pp. 463, 474, fig. 343. A. McComb, "Bacchiacca", *The Art Bulletin*, 1926, VIII, p. 157. A. Scharf, "Bacchiacca: A New Contribution", *The Burlington Magazine*, Febr. 1937, p. 36.   *Paintings and Sculptures from the Kress Collection* National Gallery of Art, Washington, D.C., 1951, Cat. No. 54.   *The Samuel H. Kress Collection in the Isaac Delgado Museum*, New Orleans, 1953, p. 36, ill. p. 37.

PORTRAIT OF AN OLD MAN   Fig. 40.
Gemäldegalerie Kassel.

PANEL: 37⅞ × 28⅔ inches.

DATE: 1525–1530.

DESCRIPTION: This portrait is closely related in composition and style to the *Portrait of a Young Lute Player*. Schmidt-Degener has identified it as a Portrait of the Pope Adrian VI. Acquired by the Museum in England in 1888/89.

BIBLIOGRAPHY: A. Venturi, *Storia dell'Arte Italiana*, 1925, IX, pt. 1, p. 474, note 1. B. Berenson, *Italian Pictures of the Renaissance*, 1932, p. 35. A. Scharf, "Bacchiacca: A New Contribution", *The Burlington Magazine*, 1937, p. 65. F. Schmidt-Degener, "An unidentified Portrait of Pope Adrian VI by Bacchiacca", *The Burlington Magazine*, 1939, p. 234. *Katalog der Staatlichen Gemäldegalerie zu Kassel*, 1958.

PORTRAIT OF A LADY WITH A NOSEGAY   Fig. 41.
Isabella Stewart Gardner Museum, Boston.

PANEL: 22 × 16½ inches.

DATE: 1523–1525.

DESCRIPTION: The composition shows the influence of Andrea del Sarto. The Lady wears a green dress with red sleeves and white trimmings. Over her hair is a green scarf with violet ribbons. Around her throat is a golden necklace. She holds flowers in her right hand. Formerly Rankin, New York; Coppoli, Florence.

BIBLIOGRAPHY: B. Berenson, *Florentine Painters of the Renaissance*, 1907, pp. 102–103. A. McComb, "Bacchiacca", *The Art Bulletin*, 1926, VIII, p. 150. G. W. Longstreet, *Gardner Museum Catalogue*, p. 92.

VIRGIN AND CHILD   Fig. 42.
Present whereabouts unknown.

PANEL: 23½ × 19¾ inches.

DATE: 1520

DESCRIPTION: This painting is closely related to Andrea del Sarto's composition of the same subject in the Wallace Collection, London and in the Barberini Palace, Rome. The Madonna wears a rose gown with blue sleeves. On her right knee is a green drapery. The yellow scarf partly covers the Infant's body. The hair of the Madonna as well as of the Child is blond. Formerly George and Florence Blumenthal, U.S.A.

BIBLIOGRAPHY: S. Rubinstein-Bloch, *Collection of George and Florence Blumenthal*, 1926, I, pl. 15.

LEDA AND THE SWAN   Fig. 43.
Troyes Museum, France.

PANEL: very small

DATE: c. 1520–1525.

DESCRIPTION: This little panel was formerly attributed to Lorenzo di Credi in the Museum of Troyes. Otto Benesch has assigned it to Franciabigio. Berenson rightly listed it as Bacchiacca. The same pose is repeated in three other versions of Leda by Bacchiacca all based on the famous composition by Leonardo. The landscape in the background is also typical of Bacchiacca.

BIBLIOGRAPHY: B. Berenson, *The Florentine Painters of the Renaissance*, 1907, pp. 102–103.   A. McComb, "Bacchiacca", *The Art Bulletin*, 1926, VIII, p. 165.

LEDA AND THE SWAN   Fig. 44.
Boymans-van-Beuningen Museum, Rotterdam.

PANEL: 15⅜ × 11⅜ inches.

DATE: c. 1525–1530.

DESCRIPTION: Another variation of the leonardesque composition closely related with the Leda, formerly in Böhler and Swarzenski collections. Only three children are shown seated on the ground, at the left. Formerly Auspitz, Austria; v. Beuningen, Holland.

BIBLIOGRAPHY: G. Frizzoni, "La Peinture en Europe: La Belgique", *Archivio Storico dell'Arte*, 1896, p. 400.   Crowe & Cavallcaselle, *New History of Painting in Italy*, 1908–09, pp. 443–513.   P. Schubring, *Cassoni*, 1923, No. 829, Pl. CLXXVI.   D. Hannema, *Catalogue of the Collection D. G. van Beuningen*, 1949, p. 88, pl. 79.   *Catalogue of the Exhibition "Chefs-d'Oeuvre" de Collection Van Beuningen*, Petit Palais, Paris, 1952.

LEDA AND THE SWAN   Fig. 45.
Collection of Mr. & Mrs. Jack Linsky, New York.

PANEL: 15½ × 12 inches.

DATE: around 1525.

DESCRIPTION: The pose of Leda is derived from the Dürer's engraving *The Penance of St. John Chrysostomus*. Five children play on the ground. Very pale, cool and lovely colors. Formerly Bondy, Vienna.

BIBLIOGRAPHY: B. Berenson, *Italian Pictures of the Renaissance*, 1932, pp. 34–35.   A. Venturi, *Storia dell'Arte Italiana*, 1925, IX, pt. 1, p. 474. Dr. Valentiner & Dr. Suida, *Catalogue of the Loan Exhibition "Leonardo da Vinci"*, *Los Angeles County Museum*, June 3–July 17, 1949, Cat. No. 8.

LEDA AND THE SWAN   Fig. 46.
Berenson Collection, Florence.

PANEL: 10 × 8 inches.

DATE: 1525–1530.

50

DESCRIPTION: The composition and the type of Leda are different from other versions. Only two of her children—Castor and Pollux are seated in the egg-shells at her feet. Her coif is purple pink. The backgraund is similar to that of the other versions. The colors and the surface are not so smooth as usual and the execution of the landscape is sketchy.

BIBLIOGRAPHY: B. Berenson, *The Florentine Painters of the Renaissance*, 1907, pp. 102–103.

LEDA AND THE SWAN
(not illustrated)   Fig. 47.
Present whereabouts unknown.

PANEL: $16\frac{1}{8}$ × $11\frac{1}{2}$ inches.

DATE: 1525–1530.

DESCRIPTION: A variation of the composition in the Van Beuningen collection. Formerly Böhler, Munich; Swarzenski, Switzerland.

BIBLIOGRAPHY: P. Schubring, *Cassoni*, (Apollo), 1928, p. 182.   Letter from Mr. J. Böhler, March 3rd, 1960.

BUST OF THE MAGDALEN (La Maddalena)
Fig. 48.
Palazzo Pitti, Florence.

PANEL: ca. $18\frac{7}{8}$ × 14 inches.

DATE: 1525–1535.

DESCRIPTION: She wears a red dress trimmed with leopard fur. A. McComb has found this painting over-cleaned and harsh. It is in a good state of preservation and very lovely in color and expression.

BIBLIOGRAPHY: O. H. Giglioli, "Notiziario—R. Galleria Pitti", *Rivista d'Arte*, 1909, VI, p. 150.   A. McComb, "Bacchiacca", *The Art Bulletin*, 1926, VIII, p. 154.   A. Venturi, *Storia dell'Arte Italiana*, 1925, IX, p. 470.

PORTRAIT OF LADY AND CHILD
Fig. 49.
(also called—PORTRAIT OF A COURTESAN).
University Galleries, University of Southern California.

PANEL: $27\frac{1}{2}$ × $21\frac{1}{2}$ inches.

DATE: 1525–1535.

DESCRIPTION: A young woman with reddish hair wears a cinnober red dress with green-blue trimmings. The background is grey. The painting is based on the drawing attributed to Michelangelo. Formerly Remak, Berlin.

BIBLIOGRAPHY: Inge Berge, "Un dipinto sconosciuto del Bacchiacca e il suo modello", *Rivista d'Arte*, Anno XVII, 1935, p. 85.

4*

WOMAN WITH A CAT   Fig. 50.
Private Collection, Italy.

DATE: 1525–1530.

DESCRIPTION: A young woman with auburn hair holds a domestic cat in her hands. She wears a yellow dress and a green-blue coif with red shades in the folds. Her face recalls that of the Magdalen in Pitti, Florence. Hitherto not reproduced.

BIBLIOGRAPHIE: *Catalogue of the Exhibition—Le Triumphe du Mannerisme Européen de Michelange au Gréco*, July–Oct. 1955, Amsterdam, pp. 48–49.

ST. JOHN THE BAPTIST IN THE WILDERNESS   Fig. 51.
Kunsthalle, Bremen.

PANEL: $18\frac{1}{4} \times 13\frac{1}{2}$ inches.

DATE: c. 1525–1530.

DESCRIPTION: This version of the composition is more mature in execution than the two others and must be of later date. The landscape in the background is borrowed from the engraving by Dürer *The Penance of St. John Chrysostomus*. Formerly Private collection, England; Mathiesen Gallery, Berlin.

BIBLIOGRAPHY: E. Waldmann, "Dürer's Wirkung und seine Italienischen Zeitgenossen", *Zeitschrift für Bildende Kunst*, 1931–32, 65, pp. 208–210. Gazzanti, ed., *Enciclopedia della Pittura Italiana*, 1950, (A-G).

MADONNA WITH ST. ELISABETH AND ST. JOHN   Fig. 52.
Private, Collection Florence.

PANEL: ca. $47\frac{1}{2} \times 35\frac{3}{4}$ inches.

DATE: c. 1525–1530.

DESCRIPTION: One of the several versions of the compositions. The Infant St. John seated at the Virgin's feet is a repetition from the Madonna, formerly in the Doetsch collection, and the Madonna in the Wiesbaden Gallery. The colors are smooth and metallic. Pale grey flesh tone highlighted with pale pink. The dress of the Madonna is soft purple; the mantle green-blue.

BIBLIOGRAPHY: G. Poggi, "Di una Madonna di Bacchiacca attribuito a Raffaelo", *Monatshefte*, 1908, pp. 275–280.   A. McComb, "Bacchiacca", *The Art Bulletin*, 1926, VIII, p. 154.

MADONNA WITH ST. ELISABETH AND ST. JOHN Fig. 53.
Private collection, Florence.

DESCRIPTION: A repetition of the Wildenstein and Fig. 52 Madonnas with different figures in the background.

BIBLIOGRAPHY: G. Poggi, "Di una Madonna di Bacchiacca attribuito a Raffaelo", *Monatshefte*, 1908, pp. 275–280.   M. Tinti, *Il Bacchiacca*, 1925, Pl. 1.   A. McComb, "Bacchiacca", *The Art Bulletin*, 1926, VIII, p. 154.

MADONNA WITH ST. ELISABETH AND ST. JOHN Fig. 54.
Wildenstein Galleries, New York.

PANEL: $48\frac{1}{4} \times 36$ inches.

DATE: c. 1530–1535.

DESCRIPTION: A large and decorative composition close to the Figs. 52–53 Madonnas. Very bright in coloring—the dress of the Madonna is pink with crimson sleeves; the mantle green and blue. In the background, at the left, is a group derived from the engraving by Lucas von Leyden *The Beggars*. Formerly Serristori, Florence.

BIBLIOGRAPHY: B. Berenson, *The Florentine Painters of the Renaissance*, 1907, pp. 102–103.   G. Poggi, "Di una Madonna di Bacchiacca attribuito a Raffaelo", *Monatshefte*, 1908, pp. 275–280.   A. Venturi, *Storia dell'Arte Italiana*, 1925, IX, pt. 1, p. 474.   A. McComb, Bacchiacca", *The Art Bulletin*, 1926, VIII, p. 154.   L. Marcucci, "Contributo al Bacchiaca", *Bolletino d'Arte*, 1958, pp. 26–39.

MADONNA AND CHILD WITH ST. ANNE Fig. 55.
Collection of Earl of Yarborough, England.

PANEL: $16\frac{1}{4} \times 12\frac{3}{4}$ inches.

DATE: 1520–1530.

DESCRIPTION: Inspired by Fra Bartolommeo's *Madonna Enthroned* at S. Marco Museum in Florence, this beautiful and monumental composition again demonstrates the pastiche method of Bacchiacca and shows a group of the Madonna and Child being a combination of two adoptations: the Madonna almost directly repeated after Fra Bartolommeo and the Child taken from Andrea del Sarto. The Infant St. John at the bottom left corner is a repetition from three other compositions of Bacchiacca. The bas-reliefs at both sides of the throne are derived from Centauromachy and Nereid sarcophagi which he must have known through some drawings. Lionello Venturi considered this painting one of the best among Bacchiacca's compositions. Formerly in Delaroff collection, Russia.

BIBLIOGRAPHY: B. Berenson, *The Florentine Painters of the Renaissance*, 1907, pp. 102–103.   L. Venturi, "Saggio Sulle Opere d'Arte Italiana a Pietroburga, *L'Arte*, 1915, p. 130.   Phillis Pray Bober, *Drawings after the antique by Amico Aspertini*, London, 1957.

GIRL WITH A LUTE   Fig. 56.
Collection of the Count Contini-Bonacossi, Florence.

CANVAS: 31 × 25 inches.

DATE: 1525–1530.

DESCRIPTION: Strong in coloring. She wears a dark bodice with ample purple pink sleeves and a large dark turban with a flower. The very white face has a tense and watchful expression. Despite the difference in time of the execution, this portrait is somewhat similar to that of the *Young Lute Player* in the Isaac Delgado Museum, New Orleans. Formerly Fischer, New York.

BIBLIOGRAPHY: A. Venturi, *Storia dell'Arte Italiana*, 9, 1925, p. 464. E. Cecchi, "Dipinti del Bacchiacca", *Pinacotheca*, 1928–1929, pp. 88–92.

PORTRAIT OF THE PHILOSOPHER ORIGENE   Fig. 57.
SALECCHI
Present whereabouts unknown. Sent to New York in 1956.

PANEL: $32\frac{1}{4}$ × $21\frac{1}{2}$ inches.

DATE: 1533.

DESCRIPTION: Origene Salecchi wears a pink gown and a black mantle and hat. On the scroll in his right hand is written: Peripateticarum rerum perscrutator.... The name of the sitter and the date are written in the left top corner of the panel. An extremely interesting example of the portraiture by Bacchiacca revealing strong Northern influence. Formerly Volterra, Florence.

BIBLIOGRAPHY: L. Marcucci, "Contributo al Bacchiaca", *Bolletino d'Arte*, 1958, pp. 26–39.

HOLY FAMILY   Fig. 58.
Private Collection, Florence.

PANEL: tondo, diam. 40 inches.

DATE: 1530's

DESCRIPTION: A lovely copy of Michelangelo's work. The landscape in the background is very typical of Bacchiacca. Beautiful color-scheme. Formerly Constantini, Paris.

BIBLIOGRAPHY: O. Giglioli, "Bacchiacca che copia Michelangelo", *Rivista d'Arte*, XIX, 44 sgg.

PORTRAIT OF A SAVANT   Fig. 59.
Private collection, New York.

PANEL: 13 × 10 inches.

DATE: c. 1525–1535.

DESCRIPTION: A man wearing a brown gown and a black cap looks at
the spectator over his left shoulder. He holds a piece of a manuscript
in his hands. His elbow rests on the parapet. Grey background. Formerly
J. H. McFadden, Jr., U.S.A.

BIBLIOGRAPHY: *Sale Catalogue of J. H. McFadden, Jr. at Parke-Bernet*, I. II.
1956.

CHRIST BEFORE PILATE   Fig. 60.
Uffizi, Florence.

PANEL: 19⅝ × 16⅛ inches.

DATE: c. 1535–1540.

DESCRIPTION: This interesting little painting shows the blend of Northern
engravings with the dramatic element borrowed from Michelangelo.
The composition is derived from Dürer's engraving of the same subject.
The man who stands behind Christ has the face of "L'âme damnée".
The type of Christ is Northern. Strong coloring.

BIBLIOGRAPHY: B. Berenson, *Italian Pictures of the Renaissance*, 1932, pp.
34–35.   L. Marcucci, "Contributo al Bacchiacca", *Bolletino d'Arte*, 1958,
pp. 26–39.

AGONY IN THE GARDEN   Fig. 61.
Lycett Green Collection, City of York Art Gallery, England.

PANEL: tondo, diam. 38 inches.

DATE: c. 1535–1540.

DESCRIPTION: This painting has a strong Northern style created by the
use of engravings of Lucas von Leyden and Dürer. Formerly S. Francesco Masi, Italy; Sellar, England; Ingram, England.

BIBLIOGRAPHY: *National Art Collection Fund*, Annual report, 1955, p. 38.
Hans Hess, *Catalogue of the Inauguration Exhibition*, The Lycett Green
Collection, City of York Gallery, 1955, No. 53.

THE SAINT FAMILY IN THE LANDSCAPE   Fig. 62.
Present whereabouts unknown

PANEL: 26½ × 19 inches.

DATE: c. 1535–1540.

DESCRIPTION: A very characteristic work of Bacchiacca with the Madonna taken from the Raphael's *Virgin with a Palm Tree* and the Child copied from Michelangelo's *Holy Family*. The landscape is very detailed and fantastic. This painting is described as *Adoration* in the catalogue of the Doetsch collection. Formerly Doetsch, London, R. Langton-Douglas, England.

BIBLIOGRAPHY: *Catalogue of Collection of O. Doetsch Esq.* London, 1895, Sale no. 110.   A. Scharf, "Bacchiacca: A New Contribution", *The Burlington Magazine*, Febr. 1937, pp. 60–70.

MADONNA AND CHILD WITH THE INFANT ST. JOHN
Gemäldegalerie Wiesbaden.

Fig. 63.

PANEL: 25¼ × 19¾ inches.

DATE: c. 1535–1540.

DESCRIPTION: This composition is based on the engraving by Marcantonio after Raphael's *Virgin with the Palm Tree*. The landscape in the background is derived from Northern engravings. Formerly Gernisch, Germany.

BIBLIOGRAPHY: A. McComb, "Bachiacca", *The Art Bulletin*, 1926, VIII, p. 162.   *Gemäldegalerie Wiesbaden*, Amtlicher Katalog, 1937, p. 6.

MADONNA AND CHILD WITH THE INFANT ST. JOHN
Collection of J. H. M. van Rooy, the Hague.

Fig. 64.

PANEL: 24½ × 19½ inches.

DATE: c. 1535–1540.

DESCRIPTION: The repetition of the Wiesbaden Madonna with the landscape derived from the Dürer's engraving *The Prodigal Son*. Formerly Doetsch, England.

BIBLIOGRAPHY: G. Poggi, "Di una Madonna di Bacchiacca attribuito a Raffaelo", *Monatshefte*, 1908, pp. 275–280.   *Catalogue of Collection of Pictures of Old Masters of O. Doetsch, Esq.*, London, 1895, p. 32. A. McComb, "Bacchiacca", *The Art Bulletin*, 1926, VIII, p. 158.

YOUNG ST. JOHN THE BAPTIST
Collection of Mr. & Mrs. O'Connor Lynch, New York.

Fig. 65.

PANEL: 20½ × 27 inches.

DATE: c. 1530–1540.

DESCRIPTION: A leonardesque imitation. The Saint wears a red cloak and a spotted fur over his right shoulder. The background is greenish grey, skinned and showing the brown underpaint. Fleshy torso with heavy shoulders and neck is typical of Bacchiacca's male nude figures. The flesh tone is pinkish; the modelling of the face is similar to that of the *Christ Carrying the Cross* in the Drury-Lowe collection. St. John wears a wreath of thickly painted wine leaves which suggests an earlier attempt to turn the figure of the Saint into that of Bacchus. It is possible that the cross was then turned into a tyrsus. The attribution to Bacchiacca was first made by Mr. Lynch. Professor Enzo Carli of the Pinacotheca of Siena has also recognized it as Bacchiacca.

BIBLIOGRAPHY: *Bacchiacca and His Friends*, An Exhibition Presented by The Baltimore Museum of Art, Jan 10–Febr. 19, 1961, *Catalogue*, p. 37.

MADONNA AND CHILD   Fig. 66.
The Baltimore Museum of Art, Baltimore.

PANEL: 33 × 26 inches.

DATE: 1540–1557.

DESCRIPTION: This work belongs to michelangelesque works of Bacchiacca. Very intensive coloring—the Madonna wears a purple pink tunic and green mantle. Over her hair is a violet-brown kershief. Flesh tone is very light. The landscape is greenish blue. The same composition was repeated by Granacci and Bacchiacca himself and is possibly based on the lost cartoon by Michelangelo. Formerly Crespi, Milan, Heilbuth, Hearst.

BIBLIOGRAPHY: A. Venturi, "La Galeria Crespi in Milano", *L'Arte*, 1900, p. 211.   B. Berenson, *The Florentine Painters of the Renaissance*, 1907, p. 103.   *Galeria Crespi, Sale Catalogue*, Galerie Georges Petit, June 4, 1914, No. 2.   *Danish Museum of Fine Arts*, Copenhagen, 1920, p. 26, no. 19.   A. Venturi, *Storia dell'Arte Italiana*, 1925, IX, pp. 473, 475. A. McComb, "Bacchiacca", *The Art Bulletin*, 1926, VIII, p. 158. B. Berenson, *Italian Pictures of the Renaissance*, 1932, p. 35.   *Art Objects and Furnishings from the W. R. Hearst Collection*, Catalogue Raisonné, Hammer Galleries, N.Y. 1941, No. 52. 36, p. 15.   *The Baltimore Museum of Art News, XXIV, Fall 1960.*

MADONNA AND CHILD   Fig. 67.
Collection of Mr. & Mrs. Jack Linsky, New York.

PANEL: 34 × 26¾ inches.

DATE: c. 1533–1540.

DESCRIPTION: A leonardesque variation of the Madonna in the Baltimore Museum. The Madonna wears a crimson dress and a green mantle. Her auburn hair is uncovered. The background shows grey rocks. Formerly Sir H. Michelis, H. de Kernavanois.

BIBLIOGRAPHY: *The Sale Catalogue of the Collection of Viscountess H. de Kernavanois.*

HOLY FAMILY   Fig. 68.
Ambrosiana, Milan.

PANEL: 47⅞ × 34⅞ inches.

DATE: c. 1533–1540.

DESCRIPTION: Morelli assigned this painting to the last period of Bacchiacca's activity. It shows the mature style of the master who used for this composition either a drawing done after Leonardo's *Virgin of the Rocks* or derived it from Perugino's *Madonna* in the Nancy Gallery, France. The color-scheme is typical of Bacchiacca. The Madonna wears a pink garment with yellow sleeves; St. Joseph is garbed in violet tunic and a blue under-habit embroidered with gold. The plants, flowers and berries are painted with great skill. Formerly Cook, England; Brivio, Milan.

BIBLIOGRAPHY: G. Morelli, *Critical Studies of Italian Painters*, 1900, pp. 101–113.   T. Borenius, *Catalogue of the Collection of Sir Herbert Cook in Richmond at Doughty*, 1913, Vol. I. p. 45, No. 39.   W. Bombe, *Perugino*, 1914, p. 153.   A. McComb, "Bacchiacca", *The Art Bulletin*, 1926, VIII, p. 161.   W. Suida, *Leonardo und Sein Kreis*, 1929, p. 245.

DECAPITATION OF ST. JOHN THE BAPTIST   Fig. 69.
Staatliche Museen, Berlin.

PANEL: 66½ × 57½ inches.

DATE: 1535–1545.

DESCRIPTION: The composition is borrowed from the Dürer's woodcut of the same subject. The colors are cool and bright. The figure of Salome is michelangelesque.

BIBLIOGRAPHY: D. von Hadeln, "Bilder Romaninos und Bacchiacca's und ihre Beziehung zu Dürer", *Jahrbuch d. kön. preuß. Kunstsammlung*, 1908, 29, pp. 247–251.   H. Voss, *Spätmalerei der Renaissance in Rom und Florenz*, 1920, p. 161.   A. McComb, "Bacchiacca", *The Art Bulletin*, 1926, VIII, 150.

MOSES STRIKING THE ROCK
Present Whereabouts unknown.

Fig. 70.

PANEL: 42 × 30 inches.

DATE: 1545–1555.

DESCRIPTION: This panel was formerly attributed to Andrea del Sarto and Dürer. It belongs, undoubtedly, to the series of paintings depicting the Story of Moses. The familiar figures of Dalilah from the *Portrait of the Young Lute Player*, of the Old Woman from the *Beggars* by Lucas von Leyden and many others are placed around the figure of Moses. There is a drawing in the Uffizi—"Studi di Teste" (black chalk) which is one of the sketches for this picture. The figure of the groveling man who drinks water in the foreground at the right made Friedman suppose that this picture was painted earlier than *The Gathering of Manna* in which the same figure is repeated mechanically. Although different in composition and figures this panel is related in feeling to the picture of the same subject by Lucas von Leyden in the Museum of Fine Arts, Boston. Formerly Prince Giovanelli, Venice.

BIBLIOGRAPHY: G. Morelli, *Critical Studies of Italian Painters*, 1900, p. 108. N. Barbantini, "La Quadreria Giovanelli", *Emporium*, 1908, pp. 183–205. A. McComb, "Bacchiacca", *The Art Bulletin*, 1926, p. 162. H. Friedman, "Bacchiacca's Gathering of Manna in the National Gallery", *Gazette des Beaux-Arts*, 31–32, pp. 151–158.

THE GATHERING OF MANNA
The National Gallery of Art, Washington, D.C.

Fig. 71.

PANEL: 44 × 37½ inches.

DATE: 1545–1555.

DESCRIPTION: A monumental painting of Bacchiacca's mature period. Vasari mentioned the pictures with the Story of Moses painted for the festive decorations in 1525. They probably served as cartoons for the compositions of *The Gathering of Manna* and *Moses Striking the Rock* executed much later on panels. Manneristic and beautiful color-scheme —pink highlighted with blue; purple with green; pink with yellow. Among the crowds are many figures used in other compositions. Formerly Bardini, Florence.

BIBLIOGRAPHY: G. Vasari, *Vite*, VI, p. 454. P. Schubring, *Cassoni*, 1923, Pl. CLXXV, no. 826. A. McComb, "Bacchiacca", *The Art Bulletin*, 1926, VIII, p. 154. H. Friedman, "Bacchiacca's Gathering of Manna in the National Gallery", *Gazette des Beaux-Arts*, 1947, pp. 151–158. H. S. Merritt, *Catalogue of the Exhibition "Bacchiacca and His Friends"*, 1961, p. 32.

MADONNA AND CHILD WITH ST. JOHN Fig. 72.
Gemäldegalerie Dresden.

CANVAS: 49 × 39 inches.

DATE: c. 1545–1557.

DESCRIPTION: One of the latest and mature works of Bacchiacca. The figure of the Madonna has a monumental quality seldom achieved by the artist. She wears a rose-colored dress, a blue-green mantle and a violet kershief over her hair. The building in the background, at the left, is derived from the Dürer's engraving *The Madonna with a Pear*. The Infant St. John, seated at the Madonna's feet, is the repetition from the one in the private collection, Florence and ex-Doetsch Madonnas. Formerly Ligner, Dresden.

BIBLIOGRAPHY: *Archiv für Kunstgeschichte*, 1914, 2, pl. 85.   A. McComb, "Bacchiacca", *The Art Bulletin*, 1926, VIII, p. 153.   A. Scharf, "Bacchiacca: A New Contribution", *The Burlington Magazine*, Febr. 1937, pp. 60–70.

PORTRAIT OF A YOUNG WOMAN WITH A CAT Fig. 73.
Museum Dahlem, Berlin.

PANEL: 10¼ × 7¼ inches.

DATE: late work.

DESCRIPTION: The woman is wearing a green dress with ample long sleeves. She holds a large spotted cat in her hands. The background is grey.

BIBLIOGRAPHY: A. McComb, "Bacchiacca", *The Art Bulletin*, 1926, VIII, p. 150.

CONVERSION OF ST. PAUL Fig. 74.
The Memorial Art Gallery of the University of Rochester.

PANEL: 38 × 31½ inches.

DATE: 1550's; 1530–35 (H. S. Merritt); 1540's (Smyth).

DESCRIPTION: The composition shows borrowings from Dürer and Michelangelo and is obviously influenced by Vasari. Harsh unpleasant colors. Belongs to the late period of Bacchiacca's activity when he endeavoured to paint monumental composition not always successfully. Formerly Weitzner, New York.

BIBLIOGRAPHY: *Catalogue of the Exhibition "Pontormo to Greco" at the John Herron Art Museum, Indianapolis, Febr. 14–May 28, 1954.*   H. S. Merritt, *Bacchiacca Studies; The Use of Imitation*, Princeton, 1958.

MARTYRS OF THE ARARAT

S. Firenze, Florence.

PANEL: very large.

DATE: c. 1545–1557.

DESCRIPTION: This large panel was formerly attributed to Stradano. It shows the figures used by Bacchiacca before in very earlier works like the prostrated corpse from his *Deposition* and the groveling man from the Moses pictures which are united in one group in the background, at the left. The figure of a martyr in the center middle distance is the same as that of the "devil" in *St. Bernard's Vision*, in the Palazzo Venezia. Strong influence of Vasari combined with the curious and characteristic method of Bacchiacca always to return to his previous works, makes this little known panel very significant for the Bacchiacca's studies.

BIBLIOGRAPHY: A. Cocchi, *Le Chiese di Firenze*, 1903, pp. 34, 285. C. Gamba, "Nuove Attribuzioni di Ritratti", *Bolletino d'Arte*, 1924–25, pp. 193–217. B. Berenson, *The Italian Pictures of the Renaissance*, 1932, p. 35.

PORTRAIT OF A LADY

Fig. 76.

(also called BUST OF THE MAGDALEN)

The Springfield Museum of Fine Arts, Springfield, Mass.

PANEL: 21½ × 13¾ inches.

DATE: Late work.

DESCRIPTION: A fantastic portrait of a young woman holding a pot of flowers in her hand. Very beautiful in color—the yellow dress highlighted with pink and a blue-green head-cloth tinted with red. The profile of the Lady is different from that on the replica of this painting in the Palazzo Venezia.

BIBLIOGRAPHY: *The Bulletin of the Springfield Museum of Fine Arts*, Dec. 1954 and Jan. 1955, 22, No. 2. *Pictures on Exhibit*, 1955, XVIII, p. 55. *The Art Quarterly*, 1960, XXIII, p. 93.

SAINT SEBASTIAN

Fig. 77.

Parochial church, Borgo S. Lorenzo, near Florence.

PANEL: large.

DATE: Late work.

DESCRIPTION: The attribution of this large panel to Bacchiacca was made by Dr. Zeri. The picture shows all characteristics of the master's mature period: a bent for monumentality, the peculiar anatomy, type of the landscape and beautifully painted yellow flowers at the feet of the Saint. Borgo S. Lorenzo is Bacchiacca's birth place and he very probably honored the local church with a large altar-piece to commemorate some important event of his life.

BIBLIOGRAPHY:

SAINT LAWRENCE   Fig. 78.
Present whereabouts unknown.

PANEL: 58¾ × 29 inches.

DATE: Late work.

DESCRIPTION: The picture is evidently the right wing of a triptych. It belongs to the least known group of Bacchiacca's works of large dimensions. The variation of his own *Madonna* in Dresden is introduced as an imitation needle-work on the cassock of the Saint. Formerly Neues Palais, Potsdam.

BIBLIOGRAPHY: A. Scharf, "Bacchiacca; A New Contribution", *The Burlington Magazine*, Febr. 1937, pp. 60–70.

MADONNA AND CHILD WITH THE INFANT
ST. JOHN   Fig. 79.
The Wildenstein Galleries, New York.

PANEL: 25¼ × 19½ inches.

DATE: Late work.

DESCRIPTION: The Madonna wears a green mantle with violet shades in the folds and a green and red turban with a jewel. The background is brown-grey. The miniature version of the same figure is placed at the right in the painting *The Gathering of Manna* in Washington, D. C.

BIBLIOGRAPHY: *Catalogue of the Exhibition "Bacchiacca and his Friends"*, The Baltimore Museum of Art, Jan. 10–Febr. 19, 1961, p. 40, Illustrated on cover.

ATTRIBUTED PAINTINGS

A FLORENTINE STREET SCENE   Fig. 80.
Rijksmuseum, Amsterdam.

PANEL: 33½ × 28¼ inches.

DATE: Late work (1540–1557).

DESCRIPTION: A purely genre painting possibly painted for the Compagnia
della Misericordia in Florence. Also called the *Sheltering of Pilgrims*. The
scene is placed at the crossing of the Via della Spada and the Via delle
Belle Donne in Florence. Formerly Lord Belger, England.

BIBLIOGRAPHY: T. Borenius, "The Florentine Street Scene", *The Burlington Magazine*, 1931, LIX, p. 66.   A. Scharf, *Der Cicerone*, Febr. 1929,
pp. 115–116.   *Catalogue of the Exhibition "Le Triumphe du Mannerisme
Européen de Michelange au Gréco"*, Amsterdam, 1955, Cat. no. 14.

PORTRAIT OF A LADY IN GREEN   Fig. 81.
Present whereabouts unknown.

PANEL: 25 × 19½ inches.

DESCRIPTION: The attribution to Bacchiacca was made by Dr. Suida.
Judging from the photograph the picture is strongly re-painted and the
face of the Lady is changed. The stiff folds of the sleeves, the landscape
in the distance and the careful execution of the bejewelled turban might
have been painted by Bacchiacca at the very early date. Formerly
Pearlman, New York.

MADONNA AND CHILD WITH THE INFANT   Fig. 82.
ST. JOHN
Seminario Patriarcale, Venice. Pinacoteca Manfredini.

PANEL: 12½ × 11½ inches.

DESCRIPTION: The painting was attribute to Raphael and now to Puligo.
Venturi assigned it to Bacchiacca. The landscape is typical of this artist
while the figures are very different from all other compositions of the
same subject.

BIBLIOGRAPHY: B. Berenson, *The Florentine Painters of the Renaissance*, 1907,
pp. 102–103.   A. Venturi, *Storia dell'Arte Italiana*, 1925, IX, pt. 1,
p. 469.   A. McComb, "Bacchiacca", *The Art Bulletin*, 1926, VIII,
p. 165.

THE FLAGELLATION OF CHRIST   Fig. 83.
National Gallery of Art, Washington, D.C.

PANEL: 22 × 18⅝ inches.

DATE: 1505–1510.

DESCRIPTION: Attributed to the Umbrian School and even tentatively considered a Raphael, this picture nevertheless shows several characteristics of Bacchiacca. The suggestion of Gnoli that this is an early Bacchiacca was accepted by Borenius. The type of Christ is similar to that in the composition *Noli Me Tangere* in the Christ Church, Oxford and in the *Last Supper* in Brooks Memorial Gallery, Memphis. The form of a halo with a cross can be seen in early peruginesque paintings. The legs of Christ are an exact repetition of those of Leda in the small panel *Leda with the Swan* in the Troyes Museum. The soldier at the left appears again in the *Story of Joseph* in the National Gallery, London and in the *Baptism of Christ* in Berlin. The soldier at the right recalls the figure of one of the executioners in the panel *The Martyrdom of S. Acasio* in Uffizi. The lower part of the arch and the parapet in the background are repeated in the panel *The Vision of St. Bernard*, Palazzo Venezia, Rome. A certain skill in drawing of anatomy is probably due to some lost prototype by Perugino himself or by some of his better pupils. The coloring is bright and the landscape is still Umbrian. Formerly in Cook collection, England.

BIBLIOGRAPHY: T. Borenius, *Catalogue of the Cook Collection*, p. 63, No. 54. O. Fischel, *Die Zeichnungen der Umbrer*, 1917, p. 156. H. S. Merritt, *Bacchiacca Studies: The Use of Imitation*, 1958.

PORTRAIT OF AN OLD MAN
Hermitage, Leningrad.

(not illustrated)   Fig. 84.

CANVAS: 24 × 20 inches.

DATE: 1525–1530.

DESCRIPTION: Formerly attributed to Raphael and considered the portrait of the poet Sannazaro. R. Longhi attributed it to Ridolfo Ghirlandaio. L. Venturi and Frizzoni to Bacchiacca. The old man wears a black coat and baretta. The background is grey; flesh tones cool. The picture has suffered from the over-cleaning and restoration and the attribution to Bacchiacca is considered doubtful in the Hermitage. Formerly King William II of Holland.

BIBLIOGRAPHY: L. Venturi, "Saggio sulle opere d'arte italiana a Pietroburgo", *L'Arte*, 1912, 15, p. 130. P. P. v. Weinert, *Meisterwerke der Ermitage*, 1923, p. 39. M. I. Artamonov, *The Art of Italy of the XIV–XVIII centuries*, Guides to Exhibitions, 1955, p. 28. "Hermitage-Catalogue of Paintings" 1958, Vol. I, p. 60, No. 104 (in Russian).

PORTRAIT OF THE FLORENTINE LADY
Present whereabouts unknown.

Fig. 85.

CANVAS: 33 × 36 inches.

DESCRIPTION: The figure is half-length, lifesize and turned to the left; the right hand rests on a book of music; the landscape, seen through the window, at the left, is carefully executed and recalls the distant view with mountains and towered castle in the background of the *Preaching of St. John* in the Budapest Museum. It has been attributed to Pontormo in the Sale Catalogue of the Doetsch collection, but it is, certainly, not characteristic of him and too stiff in drawing. Formerly Duke of Roxburghe, Belgium, Doetsch, England.

BIBLIOGRAPHY: S. Reinach, *Répertoire de peintures du Moyen Age et de la Renaissance*, 1895, 2, p. 677. *Catalogue of Collection of Pictures of Old Masters of O. Doetsch, Esq.* London, 1895, Cat. No. 111.

DEATH OF ABEL
Carrara Academy, Bergamo.

(not illustrated) Fig. 86.

PANEL: $22\frac{3}{8} \times 27\frac{1}{8}$ inches.

DATE: about 1520.

DESCRIPTION: This painting was attributed to Bacchiacca by Berenson. Venturi suggests the collaboration of Bacchiacca and Albertinelli; Zeri assigned it to Albertinelli himself. This work belonged to the series of paintings depicting the Story of Adam and Eve and their Children. The suggestion of collaboration with Albertinelli explains the better quality of the drawing while the genre touches, like the raven pilfering the basket, points out to Bacchiacca. Formerly Morelli, Bergamo.

BIBLIOGRAPHY: B. Berenson, "The Morelli Collection in Bergamo", *The Connoisseur*, Sept.–Dec. 1902, p. 145. A. Venturi, *Storia dell'Arte Italiana*, 1925, IX, pt. 1, p. 464. A. McComb, "Bacchiacca", *The Art Bulletin*, 1926, VIII, p. 149.

MARCO CURZIO
National Gallery, London.

Fig. 87.

PANEL: $9\frac{1}{2} \times 7\frac{1}{2}$ inches.

DATE: c. 1520–1525.

DESCRIPTION: Probably a side panel of a cassone. Now designated as Italian School of the 16th century in the National Gallery, London.

BIBLIOGRAPHY: G. Frizzoni, "Marcus Curtius", *Archivio Storico dell'Arte*, 1895, pp. 103–105. P. Schubring, *Cassoni*, 1923, No. 827, pl. CLXXV. A. McComb, "Bacchiacca", *The Art Bulletin*, VIII, 1926, p. 157.

PORTRAIT OF A YOUNG ARTIST   *(not illustrated)*   Fig. 88.
Collection of Mr. Alfred G. Schumacher, New York.

CANVAS: $20\frac{1}{2}$ × $16\frac{3}{8}$ inches.

DATE: 1523.

DESCRIPTION: The attribution to Bacchiacca was almost certainly made by T. Borenius who catalogued the paintings of Mr. Schumacher in 1935. The young, man dressed in black, is holding a crayon. Around his neck is a chain with a medal inscribed Salaino Salbi fecit MDXXIII. Strong influence of Andrea del Sarto and Franciabigio. It has not been possible to obtain any information or a photograph of this painting.

BIBLIOGRAPHY: *Sothby Heseltine Sale Catalogue, May 27, 1939—Ten More Little Pictures*, No. 9.

MADONNA AND CHILD   *(not illustrated)*   Fig. 89.
Collection of Mr. Alfred Strauss, California.

PANEL: $15\frac{1}{2}$ × 12.

DATE: c. 1525–1533.

DESCRIPTION: This variation of the Leonardo's *Madonna Litta* was formerly attributed to Cesare da Sesto. This painting belongs to leonardesque group of paintings and shows the Madonna seated and nursing the Child against a peculiar landscape with ruins, perhaps reminiscent of Bacchiacca's stay in Rome. Her head is covered by a thick veil similar to that of the Madonna attributed to Boltraffio, in the Poldi Pezzoli Museum in Milan.

BIBLIOGRAPHY: Dr. Valentiner & Dr. Suida, *Catalogue of the Loan Exhibition "Leonardo da Vinci"*, Los Angeles County Museum, June 3–Juli 17, 1949, Cat. No. 8.

HOLY FAMILY WITH THE INFANT ST. JOHN   Fig. 90.
Present Whereabouts unknown.   *(not illustrated)*

PANEL: $33\frac{1}{2}$ × $26\frac{3}{4}$ inches.

DATE: 1530–1540

DESCRIPTION: Listed in the catalogue of the Cremer Collection under No. 354, this painting is ascribed to Bacchiacca with a question mark. It is difficult to judge a picture by a reproduction, but the type of the Madonna, the position of St. Joseph and the unusual theme of the Infant Christ crowning the little St. John with a wreath, make this attribution fairly plausible. Formerly in the Cremer collection, Dortmund.

BIBLIOGRAPHY: Catalogue of the Cremer Collection.

FALSE ATTRIBUTIONS

PRUDENTIA
Musée des Beaux-Arts, Strassburg.

PANEL: 23 × 18 inches.

DATE: not before 1525.

DESCRIPTION: A free copy of the Delphian Sybil by Michelangelo. Instead of a scroll, she is holding an orb and a mirror. She sits on the throne supported by Putties inspired by the Sistine Chapel ceiling. The colors, as described by A. Venturi, who suggested the attribution to Bacchiacca, are azurre blue, pink and yellow. The painting has a charm of a childish copy from a great work. It is called "Uranie" and attributed to Marcello Venusti in the Museum in Strassburg.

BIBLIOGRAPHY: A. Venturi, *Commentary* to "Verzeichnis der städtlichen Gemälde-Sammlung in Strassburg by G. Fischbeck", *L'Arte*, 1899, p. 471. S. Reinach, *Répertoire de peintures du Moyen Age et de la Renaissance*, Vol. I, p. 677; IV, p. 621.   Gazzanti, ed., *Enciclopedia della Pittura Italiana*, 1950, (A-G).

CRUCIFIXION
The BOB JONES University Art Gallery.

PANEL: 65⅛ × 47½ inches.

DATE: 1520–1525.

DESCRIPTION: A large and decorative composition with a landscape which shows distant blue hills, a group of trees and small figures. The loin-cloth of Christ is pale crimson. Attributed to Maso di San Frediano by Dr. Zeri. Formerly Cook, England.

BIBLIOGRAPHY: T. Borenius, *A Catalogue of the Paintings at Doughty House, Richmond*, pt. 1, p. 39.   B. Berenson, *The Florentine Painters of the Renaissance*, 1907, pp. 102–103.   A. Venturi, *Storia dell'Arte Italiana*, 1925, IX, pt. 1, p. 474.   A. McComb, "Bacchiacca", *The Art Bulletin*, 1926, VIII, p. 161.   L. Marcucci, "Contributo al Bacchiaca", *Bolletino D'Arte*, 1958, XLIII, p. 35.

SACRIFICE OF CAIN AND ABEL
Fogg Art Museum, Cambridge, Mass.

PANEL: 8½ × 13⁵⁄₁₆ inches.

DESCRIPTION: Listed as Albertinelli in the Fogg Art Museum. The attribution to Bacchiacca was suggested by Charles Loeser. The types of figures recall those of the *Death of Abel* in Bergamo, but the execution is much weaker. Abel wears a blue tunic, Cain a violet one. An orange yellow mantle lies on the ground at his side. Pale blue sky with delicate white clouds. Possibly a part of a predella.

BIBLIOGRAPHY: *Fogg Catalogue of Renaissance Paintings*, p. 87.

MADONNA AND CHILD WITH THE INFANT ST. JOHN
Present whereabouts unknown.

DESCRIPTION: Luisa Marcucci, who reproduced this painting, calls it a significant work of Bacchiacca's Umbro-Florentine period. The type of the Madonna is still peruginesque, while the landscape, seen through the window, the flowers and a half of a fruit on the parapet, recall the details in the *Madonna* by Piero di Cosimo in the Royal Collection, Stockholm. It is difficult to discern Bacchiacca's hand from this photograph. The picture was exported from Florence in 1955. Formerly Bruscoli, Florence.

BIBLIOGRAPHY: L. Marcucci, "Contributo al Bacchiacca", *Bolletino d'Arte*, Jan.–March, 1958, pp. 26–39.

IL PAGAMENTE DELLE MERCEDI
Present whereabouts unknown.

PANEL: 46 × 37 inches.

DESCRIPTION: A genre scene related in style with the *Scenes from the Life of Joseph*. The short figures and clumsy gestures have something of Bacchiacca's style, but the panel has a peculiar look of a work executed much later and recalling the genre pictures of the nineteenth century. Formerly Atri, Paris; Private collection, Rome.

BIBLIOGRAPHY: E. Cecchi, "Ancora il Bacchiacca", *Pinacotheca*, Genn.–Febr. 1929, pp. 212–215. C. Gamba, "A proposito di due suppositi Bacchiacca", *Rivista d'Arte*, 1929, XI, p. 292. R. Salvini, *Thieme-Becker...*, 1939, XXXIII, pp. 522–523 (as false attribution).

LA PARABOLA DEI VIGNAJUOLI
Present whereabouts unknown.

PANEL: 46 × 37 inches.

DESCRIPTION: A copy after a lost work by Andrea del Sarto with a Tuscan landscape in the background. There is an engraving made by Cock after Andrea and a copy by an unknown artist in Brera. Formerly Atri, Paris; Private collection, Rome.

BIBLIOGRAPHY: E. Cecchi, "Ancora il Bacchiacca", *Pinacotheca*, Genn.–Febr. 1929, pp. 212–215. C. Gamba, "A proposito di due suppositi Bacchiacca", *Rivista d'Arte*, 1929, XI, p. 292. R. Salvini, *Thieme-Becker...*, 1939, XXXIII, pp. 522–523, (as a false attribution).

SCENES FROM THE LIFE OF ABRAHAM AND ISAAC
Collection of Mr. J. H. Weitzner, London.

PANEL: 29 × 56 inches.

DESCRIPTION: Three different scenes are shown in the foreground and the middle distance. The landscape is wide and elaborately executed. This panel has many stylistic affiliations with the Borghese panel No. 463. Now attributed to Antonio di Donnino.

BIBLIOGRAPHY: F. Zeri "Eccentrici Fiorentini" *Bolletino d'Arte*, Nos. II–III, Apr.–Sett. 1962.

STORIES OF NARCISSUS AND DAPHNE
Palazzo Corsini, Florence.

PANEL: ca. 12¼ × 17¾ inches.

DATE: about 1523–1525.

DESCRIPTION: Formerly attributed to Andrea del Sarto, this painting is now listed as Vasari in the Corsini Gallery. Apollo's profile is a repetition of that of Tobias in the paintings in the Wadsworth Atheneum and in the Simon Collection. Another variation of this subject, closely connected with the picture in Palazzo Corsini, was formerly in the Benson Collection, London. It has been attributed to Franciabigio. Now both pictures are attributed to Antonio di Donnino by Dr. Zeri.

BIBLIOGRAPHY: A. Venturi, *Storia dell'Arte Italiana*, IX, pt. 1, 1925, p. 471. W. Stechov, *Apollo and Daphne*, Leipzig, 1932, p. 25. F. Zeri, *Eccentrici Fiorentini* in "Bolletino d'Arte" Nos. II–III, Apr.–Sett. 1962, ser. 4, v. 47.

PORTRAIT OF A LADY
The National Gallery of Art, Washington, D.C.

PANEL: 22 × 17 inches.

DESCRIPTION: Attributed to Pontormo. Listed as Bacchiacca in the "Enciclopedia della Pittura Italiana", 1950. The Lady is wearing a green dress and a black net over her hair. Under her left ear is a pink carnation. She holds a little terrier in her lap. The painting is not cleaned and the yellow varnish spoils the effect of colors which must be very cool. Formerly Castle Ambras, Austria; Widener, U.S.A.

BIBLIOGRAPHY: F. M. Clapp, *Jacopo Carucci da Pontormo*, 1916, Cat. No. 1. *Catalogue of the Widener Collection*, 1923, No. 2. Gazzanti, ed. *Enciclopedia della Pittura Italiana*, 1950 (A-G).

PORTRAIT OF AN UNKNOWN WOMAN
Palazzo Venezia, Rome.

PANEL: $32\frac{1}{4} \times 24\frac{1}{2}$ inches.

DESCRIPTION: This interesting portrait has been long considered a Bacchiacca. R. Longhi attributed it recently to "Amico Friulano del Dosso". Formerly Contini-Bonacossi, Florence.

BIBLIOGRAPHY: E. Cecchi, "Dipinti del Bacchiacca", *Pinacotheca*, 1928–29, VII–VIII, pp. 88–92. R. Longhi, "L'Amico Friulano del Dosso", *Paragone*, No. 131, Nov. 1960, pp. 3–9.

MADONNA
Borghese Gallery, Rome.

PANEL: $33\frac{3}{4} \times 25$ inches.

DESCRIPTION: Listed as Bacchiacca by Berenson in his *Italian Pictures . . .*, 1896 and 1904. Later he accepted the right attribution to Puligo.

BIBLIOGRAPHY: B. Berenson, *Italian Pictures of the Renaissance*, 1932, pp. 34–35. P. della Pergola, *Catalogo di Galleria Borghese*, 1959, II, Dipinti, pl. 67.

MADONNA AND CHILD
Present whereabouts unknown.

PANEL (cradled): $24 \times 17\frac{1}{2}$ inches.

DESCRIPTION: The Madonna wearing a rose gown and a blue hooded cloak stands a half-length behind a parapet holding the nude Child at her left; a glimpse of landscape over her right shoulder. This painting has been sold May 17, 1934 at the American Art Association in New York. On February 8, 1935 it has been sold again by the same association to C. H. von Hahn. It has not been possible to gather any additional information concerning this painting, or to obtain a photograph of it.

BIBLIOGRAPHY: *Sale Catalogue, American Art Association, May 17, 1934, No. 122 (not reproduced). Sale Catalogue, American Art Association, Febr. 8, 1935, No. 68 (not repr.).*

SAINT FRANCIS
Palazzo Venezia, Rome.

PANEL: $8\frac{3}{4} \times 6$ inches.

DESCRIPTION: Attributed to Bacchiacca by A. Venturi. The Saint is standing full-length, with the raised right hand and a book in the left hand. Behind him is a niche of grey marble. Cool, greyish light, deep cast shadows. Also ascribed to Dominichino. Not very characteristic of Bacchiacca. Also attributed to Il Sassoferrato. Formerly Sterbini, Rome.

BIBLIOGRAPHY: A. Venturi, *La Galleria Sterbini a Roma*, 1906, p. 139, fig. 58.   A. Santangelo, *Museo di Palazzo Venezia*, 1948, p. 47.

PORTRAIT OF A YOUTH
Louvre, Paris.

PANEL: ca. 24 × 18 inches.

DESCRIPTION: This painting has been long considered a Raphael. Morelli attributed it to Bacchiacca; Berenson to Sogliani. Gamba suggested the young Parmigianino. It is greatly spoilt by the coat of a yellow varnish which prevents one from seeing the real colors.

BIBLIOGRAPHY: G. Morelli, *The Critical Studies of Italian Artists*, 1900, pp. 101–113.   C. Gamba, "Nuove Attribuzioni di Ritratti", *Bolletino d'Arte*, 1924/25, pp. 193–217.   M. Tinti, *Il Bacchiacca*, 1925, No. 48.

MADONNA AND CHILD AND THE INFANT ST. JOHN
Palazzo Corsini, Florence.

PANEL: 34 × 26½ inches.

DESCRIPTION: Erroneously believed to be a Madonna by Bacchiacca listed by Berenson among his works. Mr. Berenson mentions a *sleeping* Child, a detail which was overlooked by all who later included this painting into the list of Bacchiacca. A. Venturi also speaks of "Bambino dormiente". L. Becherucci attributed it to Pontormo. It has been, also, attributed to Rosso.

BIBLIOGRAPHY: B. Berenson, *The Florentine Painters of the Renaissance*, 1907, pp. 102–103, No. 164.   M. Cruttwell, *Florentine Galleries*, 1907, 2, p. 85. L. Becherucci, *Manieristi Toscani*, 1944, No. 34.   S. de Vries, "Jacopo Chimenti da Empoli", *Rivista d'Arte*, 1933, XV, p. 338.

THE SAINT NUN
Borghese Gallery, Rome.

PANEL: 18 × 15 inches.

DESCRIPTION: Listed now as Maestro Toscano in the Borghese Gallery. Was formerly attributed to Vanni Raffaele. The attribution to Bacchiacca seems to be an ald one. The face of the Nun, however, reveals a certain affinity with that of the Lady in the portrait of the Widener Collection, who was also attributed to Bacchiacca.

BIBLIOGRAPHY: R. Salvini, *Thieme-Becker...*, 1939, XXXIII, pp. 522–523 (as false attribution).   P. della Pergola, *Catalogo di Galleria Borghese*, 1959, II, Dipinti, pl. 47.

SAINT CATHERINE
Städelsches Kunstinstitut, Frankfurt a. Main.

PANEL: $13\frac{1}{2}$ × $10\frac{1}{2}$ inches.

DATE: 1520.

DESCRIPTION: Attributed to Bacchiacca by Suida. Also attributed to Bartolommeo Veneto, Domenico Veneziano and Cesare da Sesto. The same woman was painted by Bartolommeo Veneto as a *Lute Player* and the *Salome with the Head of St. John the Baptist*. She wears a crimson garment and a large wreath of orange blossoms over her veiled head. The wheel is partly seen in the foreground. There are two more versions of the same painting.

BIBLIOGRAPHY: W. Suida, *Leonardo und sein Kreis*, 1929, p. 109, Note 1.

SANTA PRASSEDE
Museo Filangieri, Naples.

PANEL: $25\frac{1}{8}$ × $19\frac{1}{4}$ inches.

DESCRIPTION: A. Venturi was the only one who had included this painting into his list of Bacchiacca's works. In the Museum is has been always, and still is attributed to Aurelio Luini. The Saint is wearing a purple dress with black embroidery and the green-brown mantle. Around her head is a scarf with vividly colored stripes. There is no trace of Bacchiacca's style in this painting.

BIBLIOGRAPHY: A. Venturi, *Storia dell'Arte Italiana* 1925, IX, pt. 1, p. 474. CTI, *Napoli e Ditorni*, 1938, p. 156 (as A. Luini).

SANTA BARBARA
Hermitage, Leningrad.

PANEL: 36 × 27 inches.

DESCRIPTION: The attribution to Bacchiacca was made by Crowe and Cavalcaselle. In the Hermitage it has been formerly attributed to Andrea del Sarto and now to Puligo. She wears a red garment with a golden belt and a sable fur head-gear. Around her throat is a pearl necklace with a medallion marked with a cross. She holds in her hands a small tower. Also was attributed to Pontormo. Formerly Crozat, Paris.

BIBLIOGRAPHY: Crowe and Cavalcaselle, *New History of Painting in Italy*, 1908/09, III, p. 512.   A. Brünningk & A. Somoff, *Hermitage Catalogue*, 1891, p. 158.   *Catalogue of the Ermitage* (in Russian), 1958, I, p. 155, (as Puligo's Portrait of Barbara Fiorentina).

MADONNA AND THE INFANT ST. JOHN
Alte Pinakothek, Munich.

PANEL: tondo, diam. 44½ inches.

DESCRIPTION: Listed as Bacchiacca by Berenson, Venturi and McComb. The present attribution to Beccafumi is correct. Formerly Crespi, Milan.

BIBLIOGRAPHY: A. Venturi, "La Galleria Crespi in Milano", *L'Arte*, 1900, pp. 210–215.   B. Berenson, *The Florentine Painters of the Renaissance*, 1907, pp. 102–103.   A. McComb, "Bacchiacca", *The Art Bulletin*, 1926, VIII, p. 165.   L. Becherucci, *Manieristi Toscani*, 1944, No. 86, (as Beccafumi).

MADONNA AND CHILD
Present whereabouts unknown.

PANEL: 28¾ × 23 inches.

DESCRIPTION: Attributed to Bacchiacca and Albertinelli. The Madonna wears a green mantle with a hood and a purple dress. She is seated in the landscape with the Child in her lap. Formerly Count Castiglione, Vienna.

BIBLIOGRAPHY: *Sale Catalogue of the Castiglione Collection*, 1930, (sold as Bacchiacca).

MADONNA AND CHILD
Present whereabouts unknown.

PANEL: 31 × 22¾ inches.

DESCRIPTION: A repetition of the Castiglione Madonna with slight changes in the background landscape which shows people standing on the bridge. In the Castiglione picture the people are missing. This panel was sold by the American Art Association to E. L. Lueder in 1915. Formerly Duveen, U.S.A.

STORY FROM THE LIFE OF JOSEPH
Borghese Gallery, Rome, (Cat. No. 463).

PANEL: 30¾ × 7⅞ inches.

DATE: 1515–1516.

DESCRIPTION: Several episodes from the life of Joseph against a vast landscape. Also attributed to Pontormo, Puligo and A. di Donnino.

BIBLIOGRAPHY: F. Zeri, *Eccentrici Fiorentini* in "Bolletino d'Arte" Nos. II–III, Apr.–Sett. 1962, ser. 4, v. 47.

BIRTH OF VIRGIN
Present whereabouts unknown.

DESCRIPTION: It is hard to discern Bacchiacca's hand from the photograph. It has not been possible to find out as who attributed this painting to him. Neither the type of faces, nor the treatment of draperies reveal any affinity with Bacchiacca's work.

BIBLIOGRAPHY: Sothby Sale, May 16, 1956 (90).

SAINT CATHERINE OF SIENA
Borghese Gallery, Rome.

PANEL: 14 × 10 inches.

DESCRIPTION: This representation of the Saint Catherine, kneeling in the landscape, has been considered by Berenson as a questionable Bacchiacca. It is now attributed to Fungai.

BIBLIOGRAPHY: B. Berenson, *Italian Pictures of the Renaissance*, 1932, pp. 34–36.   P. della Pergola, *Catalogo di Galleria Borghese*, 1959, II, Dipinti, pl. 29.

PORTRAIT OF A MAN
Musée des Beaux-Arts, Strassburg.

PANEL: 11 × 9 inches.

DESCRIPTION: Bust of a man turned three quarters to the right, dressed in black. In the background a part of a brownish wall and a rocky landscape, with a lake and little figures on the road. Was bought by Bode in Milan in 1899 as Bacchiacca. Later was attributed to Beccafumi. The picture is in a very bad state of preservation.

BIBLIOGRAPHY: *Catalogue 1938 des Peintures Anciennes*, Strasbourg, No. 258. B. Berenson, *Italian Pictures of the Renaissance* 1932, p. 67 (as Bacchiacca).

CHRIST WASHING THE DISCEPLES' FEET
Musée des Beaux-Arts, Strasbourg.

DESCRIPTION: This manneristic painting, influenced by Michelangelo, was bought by Bode in Milan as Bacchiacca. Attributed now to Daniele da Volterra. Dr. Zeri assigned it to Girolamo Genga. Formerly Grassi, Florence.

BIBLIOGRAPHY: L. Marcucci, "Contributo al Bacchiacca", *Bolletino d'Arte*, 1958, XLIII, pp. 26–39 (as Bacchiacca).

HOLY FAMILY
RR Gallerie, Depositi, Florence (from the Castello).

DESCRIPTION: The Madonna and Child, with St. Joseph, St. Elisabeth and the Infant St. John, is seated in the landscape. The attribution to Bacchiacca was made by Gamba. Salvini listed it among the authentic paintings of Bacchiacca. There is a smaller version of this panel in existence.

BIBLIOGRAPHY: C. Gamba, "Nuove Attribuzioni di Ritratti", *Bolletino d'Arte*, 1924–25, 4, pp. 193–217.   R. Salvini, *Thieme-Becker...*, 1939, XXXIII, pp. 522–23.

DESCENT FROM THE CROSS
Seminario Patriarcale, Venice. Pinacoteca Manfredini.

PANEL: (ca.) 30 × 23 inches.

DATE: shortly before 1520 (Middeldorf); about 1525 (McComb).

DESCRIPTION: This variation of the Deposition is now attributed to Puligo. Merritt suggests Visino.

BIBLIOGRAPHY: A. Venturi, *Storia dell'Arte Italiana*, 1925, IX, pt. 1, pp. 453–474.   A. McComb, "Bacchiacca", *The Art Bulletin*, 1926, VIII, p. 162.   U. Middeldorf, "Sull'attività della bottega di Jacopo Sansovino", *Rivista d'Arte*, 1936, 8, pp. 245–263.   H. S. Merritt, *Bacchiacca Studies: The Use of Imitation*, Princeton, 1958.   S. J. Freedberg, "Painting of the High Renaissance in Rome and Florence," 1961, pp. 501.

PORTRAIT OF A WOMAN
Palazzo Pitti, Florence.

DESCRIPTION: This painting is attributed to Aurelio Luini in the Pitti. Gamba attributed it to Bacchiacca.

BIBLIOGRAPHY: C. Gamba, "Nuove Attribuzioni di Ritratti", *Bolletino d'Arte*, 1924–25, 4, pp. 193–217.

THE SCOURGING OF CHRIST
Musée National, Warsaw.

DESCRIPTION: This painting has been attributed to Baldassare Peruzzi, Jacopo di Barbari and Bacchiacca. Longhi and Griseri have published it as a work by Pedro de Campaña. Formerly Lachnicki, Poland.

BIBLIOGRAPHY: *Catalogue of the Muzeum Narodowe in Warsaw*, 1938, p. 4. Letter from the Professor Jan Białostocki dated June 15, 1960.

ADORATION OF THE MAGI
The Art Gallery, Glasgow.

PANEL: $8\frac{1}{2}$ × 17 inches.

DESCRIPTION: The Virgin and Child seated in the landscape with rocks and trees in the distance. The Wise Men offer their gifts. The painting was formerly attributed to Perugino and later to Bacchiacca. Berenson suggested Andrea del Brescianino. Venturi supported this attribution.

BIBLIOGRAPHY: B. Berenson, "Le Carton attribué a Raphael", *Gazette des Beaux-Arts*, 1897, 17, p. 64.   *The Catalogue of the Glasgow Museum*, 1911, No. 55.   *The Catalogue of the Glasgow Museum*, 1935, No. 214.

MADONNA AND CHILD
Present whereabouts unknown.

DESCRIPTION: This painting was reproduced in the News Paper SUN, January 11, 1935 and belonged in this time to Arnaud Collection. The Madonna is seated, knee-length, turned to the right and holding the nude Infant Christ in Her lap. Behind them is a dark wall, with a window at the right through which the rocky landscape is seen. It is impossible to judge the painting from this photograph. Formerly L. Arnaud, U.S.A.

APOLLO AND MARSYAS
Hermitage, Leningrad.

CANVAS: transferred from a panel. Painted as a cover of a musical instrument. 19 × 47 inches.

DESCRIPTION: Schubring listed it as Bacchiacca. In the Hermitage— École de Parmigianino. Was attributed to Correggio, Primaticcio and the Unknown artist of the Parma School, XVI century. Formerly Litta, Milan.

BIBLIOGRAPHY: A. McComb, *Agnolo Bronzino*, 1928, p. 106.   P. Schubring, *Cassoni*, 1923, p. 406.   *Catalogue of the Hermitage*, 1958, (in Russian).

LEDA AND THE SWAN
Brussels Museum.

PANEL: $39\frac{1}{2}$ × $29\frac{1}{2}$ inches.

DESCRIPTION: Attributed to Franciabigio by Frizzoni. Crowe and Cavalcaselle called it "a poor school piece by Bacchiacca". The landscape in the background is possibly by him. The figure of Leda and the four children, playing on the ground, are softer and more graceful than those by Bacchiacca in his other versions of the same theme. Freedberg has assigned it to A. del Sarto.

80

BIBLIOGRAPHY: G. Frizzoni, "La peinture en Europe; La Belgique par G. Lafenestre", *Archivio Storico dell'Arte*, 1896, p. 400. S. J. Freedberg, *Andrea del Sarto*, 1965, Vol. II, p. 216.

ADORATION OF THE MAGI
Brooks Memorial Art Gallery, Memphis, Tennessy.

PANEL: $40\frac{1}{2} \times 31\frac{3}{8}$ inches.

DATE: 1520–1530

DESCRIPTION: Berenson attributed this painting to Bacchiacca and pointed out that he used a cartoon by Fra Bartolommeo. Merritt suggested the young Vasari; Freedberg Puligo. It is strongly colored—the Madonna wears a red dress and a blue mantle embroidered with gold and lined with yellow; St. Joseph has a green robe and an orange mantle; the Magi are garbed in brown and yellow and blue with pink. The figure of a young man, seen from the back, at the left foreground, is copied from that of the Raphael's *Adoration* in the Vatican. It is one of these eclectic paintings which could be attributed to any of the minor followers of Andrea del Sarto and Fra Bartolommeo. Formerly Crespi, Milan; Habicht, Cassel.

BIBLIOGRAPHY: B. Berenson, *The Florentine Painters of the Renaissance*, 1907, pp. 102–103. A. Venturi, *Storia dell'Arte Italiana*, 1925, X, pt. 1, p. 464. A. McComb, "Bacchiacca", *The Art Bulletin*, 1926, VIII, p. 162.

BUST OF A WOMAN WITH FANTASTIC HEADDRESS AND COLLAR
Czartarsysky Gallery, Cracow.

PANEL: $16\frac{1}{2} \times 12\frac{1}{2}$ inches.

DESCRIPTION: The painting has been attributed to Vasari by Ochenkowski who pointed out to the similarity to the drawing in the Uffizi after which the *Portrait of Courtesan* by Bacchiacca has been also painted. This panel is in type of the face even closer to the drawing. The cupid is missing. She is wearing a blue-violet dress. The background is black; the flesh tone rose pink; the hair yellowish.

BIBLIOGRAPHY: A Letter from the Assistant Curator of the Czartoryski Gallery, Miss Anna Rożycka—Bryzek, dated January 5, 1961.

ADORATION OF THE SHEPHERDS
Phoenix Art Museum, Arizona.

PANEL: $23\frac{1}{2} \times 18\frac{1}{2}$ inches.

DESCRIPTION: Except the landscape in the background, influenced by the Northern engravings, there nothing especially characteristic of Bacchiacca in this painting. Unfortunately, it has not been possible to obtain any information on this panel from the Phoenix Museum.

BIBLIOGRAPHY: *Sale Catalogue of the Parke-Bernet*, May 4–5, 1956.

PORTRAIT OF A MAN
Corsini Gallery, Florence.

PANEL: c. $46\frac{3}{4} \times 35\frac{3}{4}$ inches.

DATE: 1540.

DESCRIPTION: Attributed to Bronzino and to Pier Jacopo di Sandro. Assigned to Pier Francesco Foschi and called the Portrait of Bartolommeo Campagni.

BIBLIOGRAPHY: C. Gamba, "Nuove Attribuzioni di Ritratti", *Bolletino d'Arte*, 1924–1925, p. 193.   A. McComb, "Bacchiacca", *The Art Bulletin*-1926, VIII, p. 154.   J. Alazard, *The Florentine Portrait*, 1948, p. 138, Kurt W. Forster "Probleme um Pontormo's Porträtmalerei (II), *Pantheon*, Juli–Aug. 1965, p. 230.

PORTRAIT OF A WOMAN
Palazzo Venezia, Rome.

CANVAS: $32\frac{1}{4} \times 24\frac{1}{2}$ inches.

DATE: 1530.

DESCRIPTION: Once considered a Bacchiacca of a late period, this portrait is called now a work of an unknown master. Judging from her attire, this is a likeness of an English Lady. Formerly Count Contini-Bonacossi, Florence.

BIBLIOGRAPHY: A. Venturi, *Storia dell'Arte Italiana*, 1925, IX, p. 464. Siviero ed. *Catalogue of the Second National Exhibition of the Works of Art recovered in Germany*, 1950, pl. 40–42.

MARIA WITH A FEMALE ATTENDANT
Myers Collection, U.S.A.

PANEL: 21×14 inches.

DESCRIPTION: The attribution to Bacchiacca was made by Suida who assigned it to the late period. As a part of a large composition, it represents the Holy Virgin with a female attendant, on the way to the cross. The painting has been given to the Brooks Memorial Art Gallery, Memphis, Tennessee. According to the former Director of the Gallery, Mrs. Louise B. Clark, this picture has been examined by Dr. W. G. Constable and Mr. R. Leylan who have agreed that it was not a Bacchiacca.

SAINT MARY OF EGYPT IN ECSTASY WITH TWO ANGELS
Present whereabouts unknown.

PANEL: 26½ × 16½ inches.

DESCRIPTION: The Saint is carried to Heaven by two angels. An open landscape is seen below. The painting was attributed to Bacchiacca in the Platt collection. Berenson listed it as Fra Bartolommeo. There is a similar composition by Lanfranco. Formerly Platt, U.S.A.

BIBLIOGRAPHY: Bles, *How to Distinguish the Saints in Art*, 1925, p. 105 (as St. Mary Magdalen).   B. Berenson, *Italian Pictures of the Renaissance*, 1932, p. 47 (as St. Mary of Egypt).   *Catalogue—Exhibition of Italian Paintings*, Wildenstein Gallery, Jan. 15–Febr. 15, 1947, (as The Assumption of St. Mary Magdalen).

THE HOLY FAMILY
Present whereabouts unknown.

Sold by Sothby in London in 1964.
Obviously not by Bacchiacca.

LOST PAINTINGS

"VIERGE AU SEIN DECOUVERT"

DESCRIPTION: Morelli described it as a small picture entirely repainted, of somewhat later date. The composition bears a certain resemblance to Madonna with St. Elisabeth and the Infant St. John and recalls the "Madonna del Porzo" by Franciabigio in the Uffizi. The Madonna holds the Christ to her breast; to the left is the little St. John. The landscape background is characteristic of Bacchiacca with rocks, bushes and a town in the distance. Formerly Nicole, Lausanne.

BIBLIOGRAPHY: G. Morelli, *Critical Studies of Italian Painters*, 1900, pp. 104–106.

MADONNA AND CHILD

DESCRIPTION: Listed by Berenson as Bacchiacca. Professor Zbigniev Hornung writes that this painting is no longer in the museum.

BIBLIOGRAPHY: B. Berenson, *Italian Pictures of the Renaissance*, 1932, pp. 34–36.

MADONNA AND CHILD

DESCRIPTION: It is the painting which I have seen few years ago, reproduced in a catalogue. The Madonna is seated turned three-quarters left, holding the Child. In type and attire the Madonna is the repetition of the one in the Baltimore Museum. I could neither find the catalogue again, nor gather any information concerning this painting which appeared to me an authentic Bacchiacca.

TOBIAS AND THE ANGEL

DESCRIPTION: A small painting, of which I once saw the photograph, is a combination of two variations of this subject by Bacchiacca. The Angel and the Tobias are taken from the picture in the Uffizi, while the background landscape is repeated after the panels in the Wadsworth Atheneum and in the ex-Simon collection.

THE JOURNEY OF LORENZO THE MAGNIFICENT TO NAPLES

CANVAS: ?

DATE: 1539.

DESCRIPTION: Executed for the dramatic representation by the poet Landi in honor of the marriage of Duke Cosimo.

BIBLIOGRAPHY: G. Vasari, *Vite*, VI, p. 443.

THE RETURN FROM THE EXILE OF COSIMO IL VECCHIO

CANVAS: ?

DATE: 1539.

DESCRIPTION: The companion-piece to the other painting executed for the festivities in honor of the marriage of Duke Cosimo.

BIBLIOGRAPHY: G. Vasari, *Vite*, VI, p. 443.

PREDELLA
Formerly in San Lorenzo, Florence.

DESCRIPTION: Mentioned by Vasari as "molto ben fatto" without any further comment.

BIBLIOGRAPHY: G. Vasari, *Vite*, VI, p. 454.   W. & E. Paatz, *Die Kirchen von Florenz*, 1941, I, p. 515.

COPY OF RAPHAEL'S "MADONNA DELLA CASA COLONNA"

DESCRIPTION: Waagen mentioned this painting as a fine example of Bacchiacca. Formerly Henry Danby Seymour, England (1854).

BIBLIOGRAPHY: G. Waagen, *Treasures of Art in Great Britain*, 1854, II, pp. 242–243.

SCENES FROM THE LIFE OF JOSEPH

DESCRIPTION: Rev. Sanford mentioned, besides the two pictures he bought and which are now in the National Gallery, London, two others of the same size. They were sold in 1832. Formerly Nerli, Italy.

BIBLIOGRAPHY: B. Nicolson, "The Sanford Collection", *The Burlington Magazine*, July 1955, pp. 207–213.

FRESCOS IN THE COURTYARD OF THE MEDICI PALACE

DATE: 1539.

DESCRIPTION: Mentioned by Vasari. Executed together with Bronzino and others on the occasion of the entry of Eleonora of Toledo into Florence.

BIBLIOGRAPHY: G. Vasari, *Vite*, VI, p. 87.

COPIES AFTER BACCHIACCA

BUST OF THE MAGDALEN
Palazzo Venezia, Rome.

PANEL: 22 × 18 inches.

DATE: Late work.

DESCRIPTION: A variation of the picture in the Springfield Museum of Fine Arts. Pink dress; green scarf draped over her hair. The painting is greatly damaged by dirt and yellow varnish. Now considered a copy. Formerly Hertz, Rome.

BIBLIOGRAPHY: Crowe and Cavacaselle, *New History of Painting in Italy*, 1908/09, III, p. 513. A. McComb, "Bacchiacca", *The Art Bulletin*, 1926, VIII, pp. 161–62.

ADAM AND EVE WITH THEIR CHILDREN
Hermitage, Leningrad.

CANVAS: $70\frac{1}{4}$ × 58 inches.

DESCRIPTION: Listed as a copy of the 16th century in the Ermitage catalogue of 1958. L. Venturi had referred to it as a replica of Bacchiacca's composition of Johnson Collection. Formerly Mordvinov, St. Petersburg.

BIBLIOGRAPHY: L. Venturi, "Saggio Sulle Opere d'Arte Italiana a Pietroburgo", *L'Arte*, 1912, p. 130. Hermitage-Catalogue of Paintings, 1958, Vol. I, p. 60, No. 562. (In Russian).

ADAM AND EVE WITH THEIR CHILDREN

DESCRIPTION: A copy attributed to Jacopo Chimenti da Empoli. Reproduced in the catalogue of the exhibition "The Art of Mannerism", Arcade Gallery, London, 1950. Frontispiece and No. 16 in the text.

BIBLIOGRAPHY: The above-mentioned catalogue. H. S. Merritt, *Bacchiacca Studies: The Use of Imitation*, 1958, Princeton.

ACKNOWLEDGMENTS

I express my sincere thanks to all who have assisted me in my task: museum directors and collectors who have sent me photographs and valuable information on paintings and helped me to trace lost and forgotten works of Bacchiacca.

For their advice, encouragement and friendly assistance I am deeply grateful to Dr. Bob Jones, BOB JONES University; Professor Craig H. Smyth, Institute of Fine Arts, New York; Mary M. Davis, Samuel H. Kress Foundation; Dr. Gertrude Rosenthal, The Baltimore Museum of Art; Count Contini-Bonacossi, Florence; Dr. Fiorella Gioffredi, I Tatti, Florence; Professor Vittorio Moschini, Venezia; Dr. Federigo Zeri; Miss Naomi Miller and a "Private Collector", Italy.

93

BIBLIOGRAPHY

GENERAL

Phillis Ackerman, *Tapestries the Mirror of Civilization* New York, 1933, pp. 208–209.

Jean Alazard, *The Florentine Portrait*, England, 1948, pp. 135, 138.

F. Baldinucci, *Notizie de'Professori del Disegno*, Firenze, MDCCXXVIII, Dec. IV del Sec. IV, dal 1530–1540, p. 290.

N. Barbantini, "La Quadreria Giovanelli", *Emporium*, Marzo 1908, pp. 183–205.

Paula Barocchi, *Il Rosso Fiorentino*, Roma, 1950. pp. 11, 39, 217–219; Pls. 196–201.

L. Becherucci, *Manieristi Toscani*, Bergamo, 1944, Nos. 86, 34.

Inge Berge, "Un dipinto sconosciuto del Bacchiacca e il suo modello", *Rivista d'Arte*, Anno XVII, Serie II, 1935, p. 85.

Bernard Berenson, *Drawings of the Florentine Painters*, 1903, Vol. 1, pp. 300–302; Vol. 2, p. 11.

Bernard Berenson, *The Florentine Painters of the Renaissance*, 1907, pp. 102–103.

Bernard Berenson, *Italian Pictures of the Renaissance*, 1932, pp. 34–35.

Bernard Berenson, "Le Carton attribué a Raphael", *Gazette des Beaux-Arts*, 1897, XVII, p. 64.

B. Bertoldi, *Di una nuova tavoletta di Raffaele*, Asolo, 1897.

Walter Bombe, *Perugino*, 1914, pls: 25, 31, 48, 54, 55, 127, 151, 153.

Tancred Borenius, "The Florentine Street Scene", *The Burlington Magazine*, 1931, LIX, p. 66.

Tancred Borenius, "Allegory", *The Burlington Magazine*, 1922, 40, pp. 131–132.

R. Borghini, *Il Riposo*, Florence, 1584, 1st edition, p. 447; Milan edition, 1807, p. 252.

G. Briganti, *Il Manierismo e Pellegrino Tebaldi*, Rome, 1945, pp. 107, 136.

J. Burckhardt, *Der Cicerone*, Leipzig, 1900–1901, p. 771.

Louise Burroughs, "A Painting by Bacchiacca", *The Bulletin of the Metropolitan Museum of Art*, 1939, XXXIV, pp. 97–98.

Fiorenzo Canuti, *Il Perugino*, Siena, 1931, pp. 268, 272, 317.

Emilio Cecchi, "Dipinti del Bacchiacca", *Pinacotheca*, 1928–1929, VII–VIII, pp. 88–92.

Emilio Cecchi, "Ancora il Bacchiacca", *Pinacotheca*, Genn. Febr. 1929, pp. 212–215.

Benvenuto Cellini, *The Life...*, New York, 1949, pp. 50, 60.

F. M. Clapp, *Jacopo Carucci da Pontormo*, 1916, pp. 23, 24, 78, 95, 129, 135, 157, 231.

Arnoldo Cocchi, *Le Chiese di Firenze*, 1903, pp. 32, 285.

D. E. Colnaghi, *Dictionary of Florentine Painters*, London, 1928, p. 275.

H. Comstock, "Renaissance Panel by Bacchiacca", *The Connoisseur*, 1955, p. 282.

95

Cosimo Conti, *La Prima Reggia di Cosimo I de'Medici nel Palazzo giá della Signoria di Firenze*, Nr. 116.

G. Coor-Achenbach, "The Iconography of Tobias and the Angel in the Florentine Painting of the Renaissance", *Marsyas*, 1946, 3, pp. 71–86.

Crowe and Cavalcaselle, *New History of Painting in Italy*, ed. Hutton, 1908–1909, III, pp. 443, 499, 511–513.

M. Cruttwell, *Florentine Galleries*, I. pp. 21, 125; II. p. 85.

Luciana Ferrara, *Galleria Borghese*, Rome 1956, p. 38.

Giuseppe Fiocco "Fra Bartolommeo e Raffaello", *Rivista d'Arte*, 1954, XXIX, pp. 43–53.

Oskar Fischel, *Die Zeichnungen der Umbrer*, Berlin, 1917, pp. 61, 156.

Henri Focillon, *Benvenuto Cellini*, Paris, 1910, p. 51.

I. Fraenkel, *Andrea del Sarto*, Strassburg, 1935, pp. 100–102.

S. J. Freedberg, *Painting of the High Renaissance in Rome and Florence*, Harvard University Press, 1961, Vol. 1. pp. 500–503; pls. 627–638.

S. J. Freedberg, *Andrea del Sarto*, 1965, Vol. 1. p. 168, 253. Vol. II. pp. 194, 204, 207, 216, 220, 222, 230–233, 259, 264.

Carlo Frey, ed. *Il Carteggio di Giorgio Vasari*, Munich, 1923, p. 199.

H. Friedman, "Bacchiacca's Gathering of Manna in the National Gallery", *Gazette des Beaux-Arts*, 1947, 31–32, pp. 151–158.

Gustavo Frizzoni, *L'Arte italiana del Rinascimento*, 1891, pp. 256–257.

Gustavo Frizzoni, "Giovanni Morelli e la Critica Moderna", *Archivio Storico dell'Arte*, 1897, p. 87.

Gustavo Frizzoni, "Marcus Curtius", *Archivio Storio dell'Arte*, 1895, pp. 103–105.

Gustavo Frizzoni, "Interno a due dipinti di scuole italiane nel Museo Digione", *Rassegna d'Arte*, 1906, pp. 186–189.

Gustavo Frizzoni, "La Peinture en Europe: La Belgique par G. Lafenestre", *Archivio Storico dell'Arte*, 1896, p. 400.

Gustavo Frizzoni, "La raccolta Mond ed opere attinenti alla medesima", *Rassegna d'Arte*, 1910, XI, pp. 25–31; 43–48.

Carlo Gamba, "Quadri nuovamente esposti agli Uffizi", *Bolletino d'Arte*, 1907, I, pp. 20–22.

Carlo Gamba, "Nuove Attribuzioni di Ritratti", *Bolletino d'Arte*, 1924–25, IV, pp. 193–217.

Carlo Gamba, "A proposito di due suppositi Bacchiacca", *Rivista d'Arte*, 1929, XI, p. 292.

Gazzanti, ed., *Enciclopedia della Pittura Italiana*, 1950 (A-G).

M. L. Gengaro, *Umanismo e Rinascimento*, Torino, 1944, p. 504.

Giuseppe Gerola, "Bassano, Bergamo, Instituto Italiano d'Arte Grafiche", *Italia Artistica* No. 59, 1910, p. 138.

Odoardo H. Giglioli, "Bacchiacca che copia Michelangelo", *Rivista d'Arte*, 1929, XIX, 44 sgg.

O. H. Giglioli, "Notiziario—R. Galleria Pitti", *Rivista d'Arte*, 1909, VI, p. 150.

Umberto Gnoli, "L'Arte italiana in alcune gallerie francesi di provincia", *Rassegna d'Arte*, 1908, pp. 186–193.

Hadeln, Detlev, von, "Bilder Romaninos und Bacchiaccas und ihre Beziehung zu Dürer" *Jahrbuch d. kön. preuß. Kunstsammlung* 1908, 29, pp. 247–251.

Fritz Knapp, *Andrea del Sarto*, Velhagen & Klasing Künstlermonographien, 1907, p. 85.

Lafenestre and Richtenberger, *Florence*, 1895, p. 96.

L. Lanzi, *The History of Painting in Italy*, London, 1847, I, pp. 93, 166.

Lazareff, Vittore, "Una Madonna del Bacchiacca", *L'Arte*, 1923, 26, pp. 86–88.
Alfredo Lensi, *Palazzo Vecchio*, Firenze, 1929, pp. 128, 136, 188, 345.
E. v. Liphart, *"Les anciennes écoles de peinture dans les palais et collections privées russes. La peinture italienne*, 1909, p. 28.
Roberto Longhi, "A Proposito dell'Inizio pittorico di Michelangelo", *Le Arti*, 1942, IV, p. 136.
Roberto Longhi, "L'Amico Friulano del Dosso", *Paragone*, 1960, No. 131, pp. 3–9.
Fritz Lugt, "Man and Angel", *Gazette des Beaux-Arts*, 1944, 24, pp. 325–326.
L. Magagnato, "Il Museo Civico di Bassano del Grappa", *Emporium*, 1953, XVIII, p. 26.
C. van Mander, *Le Livre des Peintres*, 1884, I, p. 138.
J. Manilli, *Villa Borghese fuori di Porta Pinciana*, Roma, 1650, pp. 111–112.
Luisa Marcucci, "Contributo al Bacchiacca", *Bolletino d'Arte*, 1958, IV, pp. 26–39.
R. van Marle, *The Development of the Italian Schools of Painting*, The Hague, 1933, XIV, p. 399.
Arthur McComb, "Francesco Ubertini (Bacchiacca)", *The Art Bulletin*, 1926, VIII, pp. 141–167.
H. S. Merritt, *Bacchiacca Studies; The Use of Imitation*, A Dissertation, Princeton, 1958.
U. Middeldorf, "Sull'attività della bottega di Jacopo Sansovino", *Rivista d'Arte*, 1936, 8, pp. 245–263.
G. Morelli, *Critical Studies of Italian Painters*, London, 1900, Vol. I, pp. 101–113; Vol. II. p. 261.
G. K. Nagler, *Künstlerlexicon*, Wien, 1924, Vol. 21, pp. 410–411.
B. Nicolson, "The Sanford Collection", *The Burlington Magazine*, July 1955, pp. 207–213.
C. Norris, "The Museo Filangieri", *The Burlington Magazine*, 1944, 84, pp. 72, 75.
Richard Offner, *Bacchiacca 1494–1557, The Blessed Virgin, the Child and the little St. John*, New York, Fearon Galleries publ. 1925.
Walter and Elisabeth Paatz, *"Die Kirchen von Florenz*, 1941, Band II, p. 515.
Andreas Pigler, *Barockthemen*, 1956, I. pp. 60, 86; II. p. 70.
G. Poggi, "Di una Madonna di Bacchiacca attribuito a Raffaelo", *Monatshefte*, 1908, pp. 275–280.
S. Reinach, *Répertoire de peintures du Moyen Age et de la Renaissance*, 1905–23, Vol. I., p. 677; Vol. II. p. 677; Vol. IV, p. 621.
A. v. Reumont, *Andrea del Sarto; Sein Leben und seine Werke*, Leipzig, 1835, pp. 133, 137, 138.
F. B. Robinson, "A Sixteenth Century Panel Painting in the Springfield Museum of Fine Arts", *The Art Quarterly*, 1955, p. 99.
G. Rosenthal, "Bacchiacca—A Mannerist with Perfect Manners", *The Art News*, Jan. 1961.
G. Rosenthal, "Il Bacchiacca at Baltimore", *The Connoisseur*, Jan. 1962, pp. 58–63.
R. Salvini, "Francesco Ubertini", *Thieme-Becker Lexicon*, 1939, XXXIII, pp. 522–523.
Alfred Scharf, *Der Cicerone*, 1929, pp. 115–116.
Alfred Scharf, "Bacchiacca: A New Contribution", *The Burlington Magazine*, Febr. 1937, pp. 60–70.
F. Schmidt-Degener, "About the Bacchiacca's Portrait of an Old Man", *The Burlington Magazine*, 1939, 74, pp. 234–239.

P. Schubring, *Cassoni*, Leipzig, 1923, pp. 65, 90, 174, 204–205, 403–406.
P. Schubring, "New Cassone Panels", *Apollo*, May 1926; March 1927; April 1927; Oct. 1928.
P. Schubring, *Die Kunst der Hochrenaissance*, 1926, pp. 57, 589.
W. Stechov, "Shooting at Father's Corpse", *The Art Bulletin*, 1942, 24, pp. 213–225.
W. Stechov, *Apollo und Daphne*, Leipzig, 1932, p. 25.
W. Suida, *Leonardo und Sein Kreis*, München, 1929, pp. 97, 68, 109; pls. 166, 167.
A. Cameron Taylor, "On Christ carrying the Cross", *The Connoisseur*, Oct. 1903, p. 89.
Mario Tinti, "Il Bacchiacca e i suoi arazzi", *Dedaio*, 1920, pp. 803–817.
Mario Tinti, *Il Bacchiacca*, Firenze, 1925.
G. Vasari, *Vite*, ed. Milanesi, 1878/82, Vols: III, V, VI.
Adolfo Venturi, *Storia dell'Arte Italiana*, 1925, IX, pt. 1. pp. 453–474.
Adolfo Venturi, "La Galleria Crespi in Milano", *L'Arte*, 1900, pp. 210–215.
Adolfo Venturi, "Verzeichnis der städtlichen Gemälde-Sammlung in Strassburg, Strassburg 1899" (by G. Fischbach), *L'Arte*, 1899, p. 471.
Adolfo Venturi, "La Quadreria Sterbini a Rome", *L'Arte*, 1905, 8, pp. 434–436.
Adolfo Venturi, *La Galleria Sterbini a Roma*, Saggio Illustrativo, 1906, pp. 133, 139.
Lionello Venturi, "Saggio Sulle Opere d'Arte Italiana a Pietroburgo", *L'Arte*, 1912, 15, p. 130.
Hermann Voss, *Spätmalerei der Renaissance in Rom und Florenz*, 1920, p. 161.
S. de Vries, "Jacopo Chimenti da Empoli", *Rivista d'Arte*, 1933, XV, pp. 329–398.
G. F. Waagen, "*Treasures of Art in Great Britain*, 1854, Vol. II. pp. 242–243.
E. Waldmann, "Dürer's Wirkung und seine Italienischen Zeitgenossen", *Zeitschrift für Bildende Kunst*, 1931–32, 65, pp. 208–210.
Woermann & Woltmann, *The Painting of the Renaissance*, 1882, p. 524.
F. Zeri, "*Pittura e Controriforma*, 1957, p. 28.
F. Zeri, *Eccentrici Fiorentini*, "Bolletino d'Arte", Nos. II–III, Apr-Sett. 1962, ser. 4, Vol. 47.

MANNERISM

Otto Benesch, *The Art of the Renaissance in Northern Europe*, 1945.
Max Dvořak, "El Greco and Mannerism", *Magazine of Art*, Jan. 1953, pp. 14–23.
Henri Focillon, *Life of Forms in Art*, 1948.
W. Friedlaender, "Die Entstehung des antiklassischen Stiles in der italienischen Malerei um 1520", *Repertorium für Kunstwissenschaft*, 1925, XLVI.
W. Friedlaender, *Mannerism and Anti-Mannerism in Italian Painting*, Columbia University Press, 1957–58.
F. Goldschmidt, *Pontormo, Rosso, Bronzino*, Leipzig, 1911.
Cecil Gould, *An Introduction to Italian Renaissance Painting*, 1957.
B. Haendcke, *Der französisch-deutsch-niederländische Einfluß auf die italienische Kunst von etwa 1200 bis etwa 1650*, Strassburg, 1925.
Oskar Hagen, "Das Dürerische in der italienischen Malerei", *Zeitschrift für Bildende Kunst*, 1918, 53, pp. 223–242.
A. Hauser, *The Social History of Art*, New York, 1951.
A. Hauser, *Mannerism*, 1965, pp. 184, 192.
T. Hetzer, "Die schöpferische Vereinigung von Antike und Norden in der Hochrenaissance", *Neue Jahrbücher für Wissenschaft und Jugendbildung*, 1935, II, Heft 4, pp. 75–92.

T. Hetzer, *Das deutsche Element in der italienischen Malerei des sechzehnten Jahrhunderts*, Berlin, 1929.

M. Hoerner, "Manierismus", *Zeitschrift f. Aest.* und allg. Kunstw., 1923.

M. Hoerner, "Der Manierismus als künstlerische Anschauungsform", *Zeitschrift für Aest. und Allg. Kunstw.*, Bd. XXII, 1928, pp. 200–210.

H. Hoffmann, *Die italienische Kunst des 16. Jahrhunderts Hochrenaissance, Manierismus, Frühbarock*, 1938.

K. Kusenberg, *Rosso Fiorentino*, Strassburg, 1931.

Roberto Longhi, *Officina ferrarese* (1934), Firenze, 1956.

F. J. Mather, *Western European Painting of the Renaissance* 1948.

Erwin Panofsky, *Idea*, Ein Beitrag zur Begriffsgeschichte der älteren Kunsttheorie. Berlin, 1960.

N. Pevsner, "Manierismus und Gegenreformation", *Repertorium für Kunstwissenschaft*, 1925, XLVI, pp. 243–262.

N. Pevsner & O. Grautoff, *Barockmalerei in den Romanischen Ländern*, 1928.

W. Pinder, *Das Problem der Generation in der Kunstgeschichte Europas*, 1928 (2te Auflage).

Alois Riegl, *Die Entstehung der Barockkunst in Rom*, Wien, 1923.

W. Sypher, *Four Stages of Renaissance Style*, New York, 1956.

R. A. Taylor, *Invention to Renaissance Italy*, 1930.

W. Wätzold, *Die Kunst des Portraits*, 1908.

W. Weisbach, "Manierismus und Gegenreformation", *Repertorium für Kunstwissenschaft*, 1928, 49, pp. 16–28.

A. Weixlgärtner, "Alberto Duro", in *Festschrift für Julius Schlosser*, Zürich, 1927, pp. 162–186.

H. Wölfflin, *Classic Art*, Phaedon Publ. 1952.

H. Wölfflin, *Die Jugendwerke des Michelangelos*, München, 1891.

I. L. Zupnik, "The 'Aesthetics' of the Early Mannerists", *The Art Bulletin*, 1953, XXXV, pp. 302–306.

CATALOGUES OF MUSEUMS AND COLLECTIONS

J. L. Allen & E. E. Gardner, *A Concise Catalogue of the European Paintings in the Metropolitan Museum of Art*, New York, 1954, p. 7.

M. I. Artamonov, ed. (Ermitage), *The Art of Italy of the XIV–XVIII centuries.* Guides to Exhibitions (in Russian), 1955, p. 28.

B. Berenson, *Catalogue of the J. G. Johnson Collection*, Vol. I, No. 80, p. 281.

B. Berenson, "The Morelli Collection at Bergamo", *The Connoisseur*, Sept. Dec. 1902, p. 148.

W. v. Bode, *Catalogue of the Otto Beit Collection*, 1913.

T. Borenius, *Catalogue of the Collection of Sir Herbert Cook in Richmond at Doughty House*, 1913, Vol. I, Italian School, pp. 45, 46, 63.

T. Borenius, *Pictures by the Old Masters in the Library of Christ Church, Oxford*, 1916, p. 36, nos. 59, 60.

T. Borenius, *Italian Pictures of the Auspitz Collection*, p. 5, 29.

T. Borenius, *Catalogue of the Collection of Lee of Foreham, London, at 18 Kensington Palace Gardens*, Vol. II, No. 88.

A. Brüningk & A. Somoff, *Hermitage*, Catalogue, 1891, p. 140, No. 40; p. 158, No. 25.

D. Hannema, ed., *Catalogue of D. G. van Beuningen Collection*, 1949, p. 88, pl. 79.

R. Langton-Douglas, *Album 1st of Viscount Lee of Foreham Collection*, Cat. 26, 2 (88).

R. Langton-Douglas, *Italian Pictures Collected by Godfrey Locker-Lampson*, N. D. No. 11, ill. p. 10.

G. W. Longstreet, *Catalogue of the Isabella Stewart Gardner Museum*, p. 92.

P. della Pergola, *Catalogo di Galleria Borghese*, 1959, Vol. II, Dipinti, Pls: 8–12; 29, 47, 67.

J. P. Richter, *Catalogue of Pictures at Loko Park*, 1901, p. 17.

J. P. Richter, *The Mond Collection*, London, 1910, Vol. II, pp. 445–448.

S. Rubinstein-Bloch, *Collection of George and Florence Blumenthal*, 1926, Vol. I, pl. 15.

E. Tietze-Conrat, *The Bob Jones Collection of Religious Paintings*, BOB JONES University, Greenville, South Carolina, 1954, p. 52, pl. 53.

O. S. Tonks, *Mr. Charles M. Pratt's Gift to Vassar College*, 1918, p. 767.

O. S. Tonks, *Vassar College Art Gallery*, 1939, p. 33, ill. p. 75, No. 11.

J. Walker, *Paintings and Sculpture from the Kress Collection, National Gallery of Art, Washington, D.C.*, 1951, No. 54.

H. B. Wehle, *A Catalogue of Italian, Spanish and Byzantine Paintings*, The Metropolitan Museum of Art, New York, 1940, p. 67.

P. v. Weinert, *Leningrad-Meisterwerke der Ermitage*, München, 1923, p. 39.

CATALOGUE OF THE EXIBITIONS

Quaderni Pontormeschi—Catalogo (Onoranze a Jacopo da Pontormo nel Quarto Centenario della Morte) Umberto Baldini; Luciano Berti; Luisa Marcucci; pp. 9, 13.

Catalogue of the Exhibition *"Chefs-d'Oevre de la Collection van Beuningen"*, Petit Palais, Paris, 1952, D. Hannema, p. 17.

Catalogue of the Inauguration Exhibition, The Lycett Green Collection, City of York Gallery, 1955, No. 53.

Catalogo—*Mostra del Pontormo e del Primo Manierismo Fiorentino*—Firenze, Palazzo Strozzi, 24 Marzo–15 Luglio 1956, pp. 114–115.

Catalogue of the Second National Exhibition of the Works of Art Recovered in Germany, Siviero, ed., 1950, Pls. 40, 42.

Catalogue of the Loan Exhibition "Leonardo da Vinci", Los Angeles County Museum, June 3–July 17, 1949, No. 8.

Catalogue of the Exhibition "Le Triumphe du Mannerisme Européen de Michelange au Gréco", Amsterdam, July 1st–Oct. 19, 1955, pp. 48–49.

Catalogue of the Exhibition "Works of Art from Midland Houses", Birmingham, July 18–Sept. 6, 1953, p. 30.

Exhibition of European and American Masters, High Museum of Art, Atlanta, 1949, Cat. No. 8.

Mannerist Drawings, Prints and Paintings—Wesleyan University, Davison Art Center, Middletown (Conn.) 1957, Cat. No. 9.

Exhibition "Pontormo to Greco" at the John Herron Art Museum (Indianapolis), Febr. 14–May 28, 1954, Pls. 4, 5.

Mostra del Cinquecento Toscano in Palazzo Strozzi, Firencze, Aprile–Ottobre, 1940, p. 27.

MISCELLANEOUS

Alte Meister aus Frankfurter Privatbesitz, Staedel Institut, Frankfurt, 1925, No. 5.
Archiv für Kunstgeschichte, 1914, Vol. 2, "Simon Collection".

Art Objects and Furnishings from the William R. Hearst Collection, Catalogue Raisonné, Hammer Galleries, Inc. New York, 1941, p. 15, No. 36, 52.

The Art Quarterly, XXIII, 1, Spring 1960, p. 93, ill. p. 97.

The Baltimore Museum of Art News, XXIV, 1, Fall 1960, ill. on cover.

Book of Illustrations, *National Gallery of Art, Washington, D.C.* p. 58, Cat. No. 272.

Catalogue of the Widener Collection, 1923, Raphael's Room, 2nd Plate.

Catalogue of the pictures in the Glasgow Art Galleries and Museums, 1935, P. 14, No. 214.

Catalogue of Collection of Pictures of Old Masters of O. Doetsch, Esq. London, 1895, p. 32, No. 109.

Catalogue "Museo Civico Filangieri", 1888, p. 345.

CTI "Napoli e Ditorni", 1938, p. 156.

Danish Museum of Fine Arts, Copenhagen, 1920, p. 26, No. 19.

Ermitage—Catalogue of Paintings, 1958, Vol. I, pp. 60, 155, (in Russian).

Fogg Catalogue of Renaissance Paintings, p. 87.

Gallery Works, Memorial Art Gallery, Rochester, Jan. 1955, p. 20.

Galleria Crespi Sale Catalogue, Galerie Georges Petit, Paris, June 4, 1914, No. 2.

Gemäldegalerie Wiesbaden, Amtlicher Katalog, 1937, p. 6.

Musée des Beaux-Arts de la Ville de Strasbourg. Catalogue des peintures anciennes, 1938, pp. 146, 148, 151.

Pictures on Exhibit, XVIII, Febr. 1955, pp. 55–56.

Preliminary Catalogue of Paintings and Sculpture, National Gallery of Art, Washington, D.C., 1941, p. 10, Cat. No. 272.

The Samuel H. Kress Collection in The Isaac Delgado Museum of Art, New Orleans, 1953, p. 36, ill. p. 37.

Rivista d'Arte, Vol. XXV, Indice Generale dei XXIV Volumi 1903–1943, L. S. Olschke Editore, Firenze, MCML. Bacchiacca—Vols: VI, XI, XV, XVII, XVIII. Bibliografia, VI, 80.

DRAWINGS

O. H. Giglioli, "Nuove Attribuzioni per alcuni disegni degli Uffizi", *Bolletino d'Arte*, 1936–37, p. 537.

L. Goldscheider, ed., *Michelangelo's Drawings*, pp. 41–42.

C. Loeser, "Disegni Italiani della Raccolta Malcolm", *Archivio Storico dell'Arte*, 1897, p. 352.

L. Marcucci, *Mostre di Disegni dei primi manieristi italiane*, 1954, pp. 55–56.

G. Morelli, *Kunstchronik*, New Series, III & IV, 1891–1892; 1892–1893.

A. E. Popham, *Italian Drawings*, 1931, Pl. 199-b.

H. Thode, *Michelangelo und das Ende der Renaissance*, 1903–1912, Vol. 3, p. 496.

C. de Tolnay, *The Youth of Michelangelo*, 1947, Vol. 5, "The Final Period", Nos. 111, 113, 114.

J. Wilde & A. E. Popham, *The Italian Drawings of the XV and XVI centuries at Windsor Castle*, 1949, p. 187, fig. 21.

101

INDEX

Ackerman, P. – 96
Adrian VI, Pope – 3, 14, 15, 49
Alazard, J. – 84, 96
Albertina, Vienna – 37
Albertinelli, M. – 11, 13, 31, 68, 73, 79
Allen, J. – 43, 100
Alte Pinakothek, Munich – 79
Ambrosiana, Milan – 26, 58
American Art Association – 76, 79
Amicis, F. de – 39
Andrea, pupil of Michelangelo – 20
Arcade Gallery, London – 93
Arnaud, coll. – 82
Art Gallery, Glasgow – 82
Artamonov, M. – 67, 100
Atri, coll. – 74
Auspitz, coll. – 50

Bacchiacca, Ubertini Antonio – 2, 4
Bacchiacca, Francesco Ubertini called
    il — birth and family — 1, 2; app-
    renticeship with Perugino — 2;
    visits Rome — 3; work for Duke
    Cosimo — 3, 4; his portraits — 4;
    And see titles of separate works.
    Bacchio, Bartolomeo detto — 1, 2, 3
Bacchiocchi, coll. – 41
Baldini, U. – 101
Baldinucci, F. – 2, 96
Baltimore Museum of Art, The – 8,
    24, 26, 44, 45, 57, 58, 62, 94
Bandinelli, B. 4
Barbantini, B. – 59, 96
Barbara Fiorentina – 78
Barbari, J. di – 81
Barberini Palace, Rome – 36, 49
Bardini, coll. 59
Barker, coll. – 48
Barocchi, P. – 30, 96

Bartolommeo, Fra – 11, 12, 25, 40, 43,
    53, 83, 85
Beccafumi, D. – 79, 80
Becherucci, L. – 77, 79, 96
Beit, coll. – 48
Belger, Lord, coll. – 66
Benesch, O. – 50, 99
Benintendi family – 16, 44, 47
Benson, coll. – 75
Berenson, Bernard – 5, 30, 31, 36, 37,
    39, 40, 41, 43, 46, 48, 49, 50, 51, 53,
    54, 55, 57, 61, 66, 68, 73, 76, 77, 79,
    80, 82, 83, 85, 88, 96, 100
Berge, I. – 19, 51, 96
Berti, L. – 30, 101
Bertoldi, coll. – 39,96
Beuningen van, coll. – 50, 51
Bialostocki, J. – 81
Blumenthal, coll. – 25, 36, 49
Bober, P. P. – 54
BOB JONES University – 16, 43, 44,
    73
Boccaccio, G. – 40
Bode W. von – 48, 80, 100
Boehler, J. 38, 43, 50, 51
Boltraffio, G. – 69
Bombe, W. – 26, 58, 96
Bondy, coll. – 50
Borenius, T. – 11, 35, 40, 45, 46, 58,
    66, 67, 69, 73, 96, 100
Borgherini, Giovan Francesco – 2, 37,
    43
Borgherini, Margareta – 2
Borgherini, Salvo – 2
Borghese Gallery, Rome – 11, 38, 39,
    41, 42, 47, 75, 76, 77, 79, 80
Borghini, R. – 28, 96
Borgo San Lorenzo, Florence – 1, 61,
    62

103

Boymans-van-Beuningen Museum, Rotterdam – 50
Brera, Milan – 74
Breschianino, A. del – 82
Briganti, G. – 96
Brivio, coll. – 58
Brompton Oratorium, London – 36
Bronzino, A. – 4, 20, 84, 89
Brooks Memorial Art Gallery, Memphis, Tenn. – 45, 46, 67, 83, 84
Brünningk, A. – 78, 100
Bruscoli, coll. – 74
Brussels Museum – 82
Burckhardt, J. – 96
Burroughs, L. – 37, 43, 96
Butler, coll. – 48

Cameron Taylor, A. 36, 99
Campaña, Pedro de – 81
Campagni, Bartolomeo – 84
Canonica della Parrochia, Asolo – 39
Canuti, F. – 2, 96
Carli, Enzio – 57
Carlo, Tommasa di, Bacchiacca's wife – 3
Carrara Academy, Bergamo – 68
Castiglione, coll. – 79
Castle Ambras, Tirol, coll. – 75
Cecchi, E. – 6, 54, 74, 96
Cellini, B. – 3, 4, 18, 96
Christ Church, Oxford – 10, 35, 67
Chimenti, Jacopo da Empoli – 77, 93
Clapp, M. – 4, 30, 75, 96
Clark, L. B. – 84
Cocchi, A. – 42, 61, 96
Colnaghi, D. E. – 96
Comstock, H. – 96
Constable, W. G. – 84
Constantini, coll. – 54
Conti, C. – 97
Contini-Bonacossi, coll. 20, 54, 76, 84, 94
Cook, coll. – 11, 26, 45, 58, 67, 73
Coor-Achembach, G. – 15, 97
Coppoli, coll. – 49
Cosimo, Piero di – 7, 22, 28, 74
Costa, coll. – 47
Credi, Lorenzo di – 50
Cremer, coll. – 69
Crespi, coll. – 57, 79, 83

Crowe & Cavslcaselle – 50, 78, 82, 93, 97
Crozat, coll. – 78
Cruttwell, M. – 42, 47, 77, 97
Czartorysky Gallery, Cracow – 83

Dahlem Museum, Berlin – 60
Danby, coll. – 89
Davis, M. M. – 94
Degas, G. – 30
Delaroff, coll. – 53
Dijon Museum, France – 10, 35
Doetsch, coll. – 52, 56, 60, 68, 102
Domenichino il, (Domenico Zampieri) – 77
Donnino A. di – 75, 79
Drury-Lowe, J. coll. – 13, 36, 57
Dürer, A. – 12, 21, 22, 26, 29, 37, 50, 52, 55, 58, 59, 60
Dvořak, M. – 99

Eleonora, of Toledo – 3, 89

Fearon Galleries, New York, – 41
Fede, Lucrezia del – 20
Ferrara, L. – 38, 97
Filangieri Museum, Naples – 78
Fiocco, G. – 12, 13, 40, 97
Fischel, O. – 1), 36, 47, 67, 97
Fischer Galleries, New York – 54
Focillon, H. – 97
Fogg Art Museum, Cambridge, Mass. – 73, 74
Forster, K. W. – 84
Foschi, Pier Francesco – 84
Fraenkel, I. – 20, 97
Franciabigio, Francesco Giudini – 1, 11, 50, 69, 75, 82, 88
Freedberg, S. J. – 36, 37, 38, 40, 42, 44, 47, 81, 82, 83, 97
Frey, C. ed. – 97
Friedlaender, W. – 6, 99
Friedman, H. – 22, 59, 97
Frizzoni, G. – 35, 37, 48, 50, 67, 68, 82, 97
Fungai, Bernardino – 80

Gamba, C. – 5, 20, 39, 61, 74, 77, 81, 84, 97
Gardner, E. – 43, 100
Gazzanti, ed. – 46, 52, 73, 75, 97

Gemäldegalerie, Dresden – 16, 24, 44, 60
Gemäldegalerie, Kassel – 14, 48
Gemäldegalerie, Wiesbaden – 52, 56
Genga, G. – 80
Gengaro, M. L. – 97
Gerola, G. 97
Gernisch, coll. – 56
Ghirlandaio, Ridolfo di – 2, 67
Giglioli, O. H. – 18, 51, 54, 97, 102
Gioffredi, F. – 94
Giovanelli, Prince, coll. – 22, 59
Giovanna of Austria – 4
Gnoli, U. 11, 35, 67, 97
Goldschmidt, F. – 99
Goldscheider, A. – 30, 102
Gould, C. – 99
Granacci, F. – 1, 2, 57
Grautoff, O. – 6
Griseri, – 81

Habicht, coll. – 83
Hadeln D. von – 21, 58, 97
Haendcke, B. 99
Hahn, C. H. von – 76
Hannema, D. – 50, 100
Hauser, A. 99
Heilbuth, coll. – 57
Hermitage, Leningrad – 41, 67, 78, 82, 93
Hertz, coll. – 48, 93
Hess, Hans – 55
Hetzer, T. – 100
Hoerner, M. – 100
Hoffmann, H. – 100
Hope, coll. – 43
Hornung, Z. – 88

Ingram, coll. – 55
Isaac Delgado Museum, The, New Orleans – 48, 54
Isabella Stewart Gardner Museum, Boston – 20, 49

Johnson, John G. coll. Philadelphia – 12, 37, 43, 93
Jones, Bob Dr. – 94

Kernavois de, Viscountess, coll. 58
Knapp, F. – 97
Kress, S. H. Foundation – 14, 40, 94

Kunsthalle, Bremen – 16, 52
Kusenberg, K. – 100

Lachnicki, coll. – 81
Lefenestre, G. – 83, 97
Lanfranco, G. – 85
Langton-Douglas, R. – 43, 46, 56, 100
Lanzi, L. – 2, 97
Lazareff, V. – 25, 41, 98
Lee of Foreham, Viscount, coll. – 45, 46
Lensi, A. – 4, 98
Leo X, Pope – 2
Leonardo, Vinci da – 18, 25, 26, 30, 42, 50, 58, 69
Leyden, Lucas van – 29, 42, 44, 46, 53, 55, 59
Leylan, R. – 84
Ligner, coll. – 60
Linsky, Jack Mr. & Mrs., coll. – 18, 26, 45, 50, 57
Liphardt, E. – 98
Litta, coll. – 82
Locker-Lampson, coll. – 43
Loeser, C. – 31, 73, 102
Longhi, Roberto – 6, 67, 76, 81, 98, 100
Longstreat, G. W. – 49, 101
Louvre, Paris – 37, 77
Lueder, E. – 79
Lugt, F. – 79
Luini, Aurelio – 5, 78, 81
Lycett Green Collection, City of York Art Gallery, England – 55
Lynch, O'Connor, Mr. & Mrs., coll. – 56, 57

Magagnato, L. – 36, 98
Mander, C. van – 98
Manilli, J. – 38, 98
Marcucci, L. – 7, 31, 37, 47, 53, 54, 55, 73, 74, 80, 98, 101, 102
Marle, R. van – 98
Mather, F. J. – 100
Mathiesen Gallery, Berlin – 52
Mc Comb, Arthur – 7, 35, 36, 37, 38, 39, 41, 42, 44, 45, 46, 47, 48, 50, 51, 52, 53, 56, 57, 58, 59, 60, 66, 68, 73, 79, 81, 82, 83, 84, 93, 98
Mc Fadden, coll. – 55

Medici, Cosimo the Elder – 3, 89
Medici, Cosimo I, Duke of Florence – 2, 3, 4, 28, 88, 89
Medici, Francesco, Duke of Florence – 3, 4
Medici, Lorenzo the Magnificent – 3
Memorial Art Gallery, University of Rochester – 23, 60
Merrit, H. S. – 7, 23, 42, 44, 48, 59, 60, 67, 81, 83, 93, 98
Metropolitan Museum of Art, New York – 12, 35, 43
Michelangelo, Buonarotti – 18, 19, 20, 21, 24, 25, 30, 42, 54, 55, 56, 57, 60, 73, 80
Michele, Michelangelo di Bernardino di – 3, 14, 19
Michelis, coll. 58
Middeldorf, U. – 10, 36, 47, 81, 98
Miller, N. – 94
Mini, Andrea – 20
Mond, coll. – 17, 38, 47, 48
Mordvinov, coll. – 93
Morelli, G. – 5, 9, 12, 26, 27, 28, 30, 31, 35, 37, 39, 41, 45, 58, 59, 68, 77, 88, 98, 102
Moschini, V. – 94
Museo Civico, Bassano Veneto – 10, 36
Museum of Fine Arts, Boston – 59
Museum of Fine Arts, Budapest – 40, 68
Musée des Beaux-Arts, Stassburg – 73, 80
Musée National, Warsaw – 81
Myers, coll. – 84

Nagler, G. K. – 98
Nancy Gallery, France – 26, 58
National Gallery, London – 3. 11, 37, 38, 67, 68, 89
National Gallery, Washington D. C. – 11, 13, 22, 27, 40, 59, 66, 75
Nerli, family – 3, 37, 38, 89
Neues Palais, Potsdam – 12, 23, 40, 62
Newhouse Gallery, New York – 16, 44
Nicole, coll. – 88
Nicolson, B. – 3, 37, 89, 98
Norris, C. – 98

Ochenkowski – 83
Offner, R. – 25, 41, 98

Paatz, W. & E. – 89, 98
Palla, G. della – 2
Palazzo Corsini, Florence – 75, 77, 84
Palazzo Davanzati, Florence – 30
Palazzo Vecchio, Florence – 29
Palazzo Venezia, Rome – 45, 48, 61, 67, 76, 84, 93
Panofsky, Erwin – 100
Pantasilea – 3, 18, 19
Parmigianino (Francesco Mazzola) – 77, 82
Patinir, J. – 22
Pearlman, coll. – 66
Penni, Francesco – 3
Pergola, P. della – 38, 76, 77, 80, 101
Perugino, Pietro – 1, 2, 10, 11, 12, 13, 17, 25, 26, 28, 35, 36, 37, 41, 47, 58, 67, 82
Peruzzi B. – 12, 81
Pevsner, N. – 6, 100
Phoenix Art Museum, Arizona – 83
Pigler, A. – 38, 41, 98
Pinacoteca Manfredini, Seminario Patriarcale, Venice – 10, 66, 81
Pinder, W. – 100
Pitti, Palazzo – 4, 18, 51, 81
Platt, coll. – 85
Poggi, G. – 39, 45, 52, 53, 56, 98
Poldi Pezzoli Museum, Milan – 69
Pontormo, Jacopo Carucci – 1, 2, 4, 8, 20, 22, 30, 68, 75, 77, 78, 79, 101
Popham, A. – 102
Prado, Madrid – 20
Pratt, coll. – 47
Puligo, G. – 10, 66, 76, 78, 79, 81, 83

Raffaele, Vanni – 77
Raimondi, Marcantonio – 45, 56
Rankin, coll. – 49
Raphael, Sanzio – 3, 13, 25, 39, 40, 56, 67, 77, 83, 89, 102
Reinach, S. – 68, 73, 98
Remak, coll. 19, 51
Renoir, P. – 19
Reumont, A. von – 37, 98
Richtenberger – 97
Richter, J. P. – 36, 47, 48, 101
Rieffel-Müller, coll. – 46
Riegl, A. – 100
Rijksmuseum, Amsterdam – 24, 66

Robinson, F. B. – 98
Romano, Giulio – 3, 12
Rooy van, coll. – 56
Rosenthal, G. – 94, 98
Rosso, Fiorentino il – 77
Rost, Johannes – 30
Roxburghe, Duke of, coll. – 68
Rozyscka-Bryzek, A. – 83
Rubinstein-Bloch, S. 25, 49, 101

Salecchi, Origene – 9, 20, 54
Salvini, R. – 7, 36, 48, 74, 77, 81, 98
Sanders, coll. – 47
Sandro, Pier Jacopo di – 84
San Firenze, Church, Florence – 23, 61
Sanford, J. Rev. – 37, 38, 89
San Frediano, Maso di – 73
San Gallo, Aristotele di – 1
San Lorenzo, Florence – 42, 89
San Marco Museo, Florence – 25, 53
Sansovino, J. – 10, 36
Santangelo, A. – 45, 77
Santa Maria dei Servi, Citta della
    Pieve – 10
Sarto, Andrea del – 2, 8, 11, 20, 25, 26,
    27, 28, 31, 36, 37, 41, 49, 53, 69, 74,
    75, 78, 82, 83
Sassoferrato, il – 77
Scharf, A. 6, 37, 40, 42, 43, 48, 49, 56,
    60, 62, 66, 98
Schmidt-Degener, F. – 14, 49, 98
Schubring, P. – 50, 51, 59, 68, 82
Schumacher, coll. – 69, 99
Seattle Art Museum – 12, 40
Sellar, coll. – 55
Serristori, coll. – 53
Sesto, Cesare di – 69, 78
Shuvaloff, Countess, coll. – 25, 41
Simon, coll. – 15, 46, 75, 88, 101
Siviero, ed. – 7, 84, 101
Smyth, C. H. – 94
Sogliani, Giovanantonio – 42, 77
Sorbelli family – 3
Somoff, A. – 78
Spengler, O. – 29
Springfield Museum of Fine Arts, The,
    Springfield, Mass. – 24, 61, 93
Staatliche Museen, Berlin – 11, 17, 21,
    44, 58
Staatsgalerie, Stuttgart – 36

Städelsches Kunstinstitut, Frankfurt
    am Main – 46, 78, 101
Stechov, W. – 17, 44, 99
Sterbini coll. – 45, 77
Stradano, G. – 61
Strauss, A. coll. 69
Suida, W. – 6, 26, 50, 58, 66, 78, 84, 99
Swarzensky, coll. – 43, 50, 51
Sypher, W. – 100

Taylor, R. A. – 27, 100
Thode, H. – 30, 102
Tietze-Conrat, E. – 16, 43, 44, 101
Tinti, M. – 6, 30, 53, 77, 99
Tolnay, C. de – 30, 102
Tonks, O. S. – 47, 101
Tribolo, F. – 1, 14
Trotti, coll. – 46
Troyes Museum, France – 16, 49, 50,
    67

Ubertini, Bastiano – 3
Ubertini, Carlo – 3
Ubertini, Ubertino – 3
Uffizi, Florence – 10, 11, 12, 15, 30,
    37, 39, 42, 43, 47, 55, 59, 67, 83,
    88
University Galleries, University of
    Southern California – 20, 51

Valentiner, O. – 50, 69
Varchi, B. – 2
Vasari, Giorgio – 1, 2, 3, 4, 5, 7, 8, 11,
    22, 28, 29, 31, 37, 38, 42, 44, 45, 47,
    59, 60, 61, 75, 83, 88, 89, 99
Vassar College Art Gallery – 11, 17,
    18, 47
Vatican Gallery, Rome – 35
Veneto, B. – 78
Veneziano, D. – 78
Venturi, Adolfo – 6, 13, 19, 21, 37, 40,
    41, 45, 46, 47, 48, 49, 50, 51, 53, 54,
    57, 66, 68, 73, 76, 78, 79, 81, 83, 84,
    99
Venturi, Lionello – 53, 54, 67, 93, 99
Venusti, M. – 73
Visino – 81
Volterra, D. da – 80
Volterra, coll. – 54
Voss, H. – 6, 58, 99
Vries, S. de – 77, 99

107

Waagen, G. – 89, 99
Wadsworth Atheneum, Hartford, Connecticut – 15, 46, 75, 88
Wätzold, W. – 100
Waldmann, E. – 52, 99
Walker, J. – 101
Wallace, coll. – 36, 49
Wehle, H. B. – 37, 43, 101
Weinert, P. von – 67, 101
Weisbach, W. – 100
Weitzner, J. – 60, 75
Weixlegärtner, A. – 100
White, coll. – 40

Widener, coll. – 75, 77, 102
Wilde, J. – 102
Wildenstein Galleries, New York – 25, 27, 31, 53, 62, 85
William II, King of Holland, coll. – 67
Wölfflin, H. – 100
Woerman & Woltmann – 99

Yarborough, Earl of coll. – 53

Zeri, F. – 61, 68, 73, 75, 79, 80, 94, 99
Zupnik, I. – 100

PLATES

Fig. 2. NOLI ME TANGERE, Christ Church, Oxford (*photo: University Press, Oxford*).

Fig. 1. RESURRECTION, Musée de Dijon, France (*photo: courtesy of the museum*).

Fig. 4. DESCENT FROM THE CROSS, Museo Civico, Bassano (*photo: Alinari*)

Fig. 3. PREACHING OF CHRIST, Christ Church, Oxford
(*photo: University Press, Oxford*)

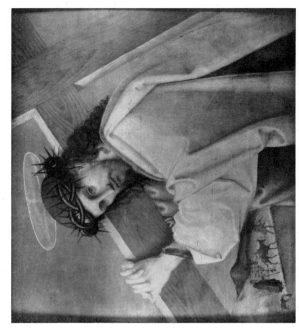

Fig. 6. CHRIST CARRYING THE CROSS, Collection of Mr. John Drury-Lowe, England *(photo: courtesy Mr. John Drury-Lowe)*.

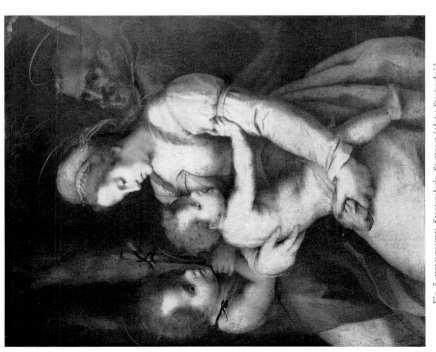

Fig. 5. HOLY FAMILY, Staatsgalerie, Stuttgart *(photo: Staatsgalerie)*.

Fig. 7. ADAM AND EVE WITH THEIR CHILDREN, John G. Johnson Collection, Museum of Fine Arts, Philadelphia
(*photo: courtesy, John G. Johnson Collection Philadelphia*)

Fig. 8. STORY FROM THE LIFE OF JOSEPH, The National Gallery, London (*photo: National Gallery*).

Fig. 9. STORY FROM THE LIFE OF JOSEPH, The National Gallery, London (*photo: National Gallery*).

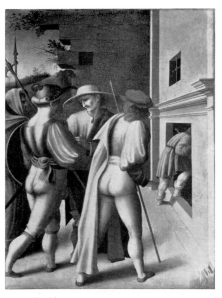

Fig. 10. STORY FROM THE LIFE OF JOSEPH,
Borghese Gallery, Rome (*photo: Anderson*).

Fig. 11. STORY FROM THE LIFE OF JOSEPH,
Borghese Gallery, Rome (*photo: Anderson*).

Fig. 12. STORY FROM THE LIFE OF JOSEPH,
Borghese Gallery, Rome (*photo: Anderson*).

Fig. 13. STORY FROM THE LIFE OF JOSEPH,
Borghese Gallery, Rome (*photo: Anderson*).

Fig. 14. MADONNA WITH ST. ELISABETH AND THE INFANT ST. JOHN,
Canonica della Parrochia, Asolo (*photo: Alinari*).

Fig. 15. TOBIAS AND THE ANGEL, Uffizi, Florence (*photo: Alinari*).

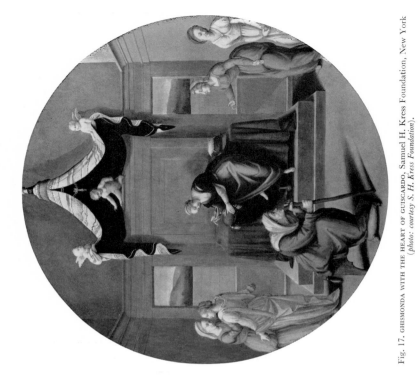

Fig. 17. GHISMONDA WITH THE HEART OF GUISCARDO, Samuel H. Kress Foundation, New York
(photo: courtesy S. H. Kress Foundation).

Fig. 16. CREATION OF EVE, formerly Neues Palais, Potsdam
(photo: courtesy Neues Palais, Potsdam).

Fig. 18. PREACHING OF ST. JOHN THE BAPTIST, Museum of Fine Arts, Budapest (*photo: courtesy Museum of Fine Arts*).

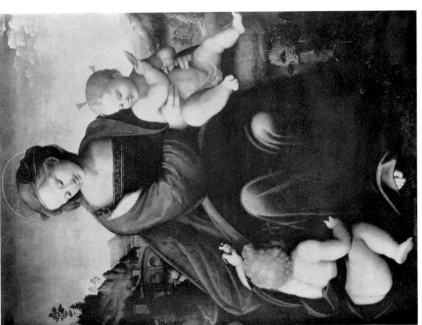

Fig. 19. VIRGIN AND CHILD WITH THE INFANT ST. JOHN, Present whereabouts unknown
(photo: courtesy Frick Art Reference Library).

Fig. 20. MADONNA AND CHILD, Hermitage, Leningrad
(photo: Reproduced from "L'Arte", 1923).

Fig. 21. SCENCES FROM THE LIFE OF ST. ACASIO (Baptism of St. Acasio and his Companions), Uffizi, Florence (photo: Alinari).

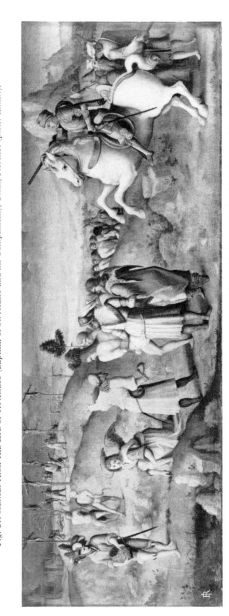

Fig. 22. SCENCES FROM THE LIFE OF ST. ACASIO (Martyrdom of St. Acasio and his Companions), Uffizi, Florence (photo: Alinari).

Fig. 23. SCENES FROM THE LIFE OF ST. ACASIO (St. Acasio defeating the Rebels with the Help of the Angels) Uffizi, Florence (photo: Alinari).

Fig. 24. THE PERSECUTION OF ST. BARBARA. Present whereabouts unknown
(photo: courtesy Mr. J. Böhler, Munich).

Fig. 25. CARITAS, Metropolitan Museum of Art, New York
(photo: courtesy Metropolitan Museum of Art).

FIG. 27.—ST. JOHN THE BAPTIST IN THE WILDERNESS

FIG. 26.—ST. JOHN THE BAPTIST IN THE WILDERNESS

Fig. 28. LEGEND OF THE DEAD KING, Gemäldegalerie, Dresden (*Photo: Alinari*).

Fig. 29. BAPTISM OF CHRIST, Staatliche Museen, Berlin (*photo: Staatliche Museen*).

Fig. 30. LAST SUPPER, Brooks Memorial Art Gallery, Memphis, Tennessy
(photo: courtesy Brooks Memorial Art Gallery).

Fig. 32. ST. FRANCIS RECEIVING THE STIGMATA,
Collection of Viscount Lee of Foreham, London
(photo: reproduced from "Album 1st Viscount Lee of Foreham Collection").

Fig. 31. THE VISION OF ST. BERNARD, Palazzo Venezia, Rome
(photo: courtesy Palazzo Venezia).

Fig. 34. TOBIAS AND THE ANGEL, Present whereabouts unknown
(photo: reproduced from "Archiv für Kunstgeschichte" 1914, 2, Taf. 117).

Fig. 33. TOBIAS AND THE ANGEL, Wadsworth Atheneum, Hartford
(photo: courtesy Wadsworth Atheneum).

Fig. 35. DESCENT FROM THE CROSS, Uffizi, Florence (*photo: Alinari*).

Fig. 36. BAPTISM OF CHRIST, Vassar College, Poughkeepsie, N. Y.

Fig. 37. BAPTISM OF CHRIST, Present whereabouts unknown

Fig. 40. PORTRAIT OF AN OLD MAN, Gemäldegalerie, Kassel
(*photo: Gemäldegalerie*).

Fig. 39. PORTRAIT OF A YOUNG LUTE PLAYER, The Isaac Delgado Museum of Art,
New Orleans (*photo: courtesy S. H. Kress Foundation*).

Fig. 42. VIRGIN AND CHILD, Present whereabouts unknown
(photo: reproduced from "Collection of George and Florence Blumenthal").

Fig. 41. PORTRAIT OF A LADY WITH A NOSEGAY,
Isabella Stewart Gardner Museum, Boston
(photo: courtesy Isabella Stewart Gardner Museum).

Fig. 44. LEDA AND THE SWAN, Boymans-van Beuningen Museum, Rotterdam
(photo: courtesy Boymans-van Beuningen Museum).

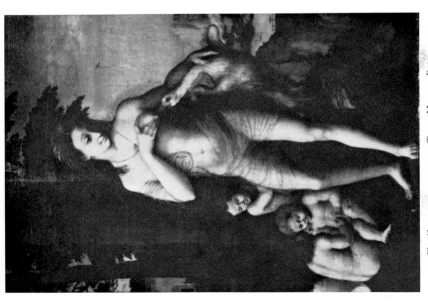

Fig. 43. LEDA AND THE SWAN, Troyes Museum, France
(photo: courtesy Troyes Museum)

Fig. 46. LEDA AND THE SWAN, Berenson Collection, Florence
(photo: courtesy Berenson Collection).

Fig. 45. LEDA AND THE SWAN, Collection of Mr. & Mrs. Jack Linsky, New York
(photo: courtesy Mr. & Mrs. Jack Linsky).

Fig. 49. PORTRAIT OF LADY AND CHILD, University Galleries,
University of Southern California (photo: courtesy University Galleries).

Fig. 48. BUST OF THE MAGDALEN, Palazzo Pitti, Florence (photo: Alinari).

Fig. 50. WOMAN WITH A CAT. Private collection, Italy (*photo: courtesy Private collection*).

Fig. 51. ST. JOHN THE BAPTIST IN THE WILDERNESS, Kunsthalle, Bremen (*photo: Kunsthalle*).

Fig. 53. MADONNA WITH ST. ELISABETH AND ST. JOHN, Private collection, Florence
(photo: reproduced from "Il Bacchiacca" by M. Tinti).

Fig. 52. MADONNA WITH ST. ELISABETH AND ST. JOHN, Private collection, Florence
(photo: courtesy Private collection).

Fig. 54. MADONNA WITH ST. ELISABETH AND ST. JOHN, Wildenstein Galleries, New York (*photo: courtesy Wildenstein Galleries*).

Fig. 55. MADONNA AND CHILD WITH ST. ANNE, Collection of the Earl of Yarborough, England
(*photo: courtesy Earl of Yarborough*)

Fig. 57. PORTRAIT OF THE PHILOSOPHER ORIGENE SALECCHI,
Present whereabouts unknown
(photo: reproduced from "Contributo al Bacchiaca" by Luisa Marcucci).

Fig. 56. GIRL WITH A LUTE, Collection of the Count Contini-Bonacossi, Florence
(photo: courtesy Count Contini-Bonacossi).

Fig. 59. PORTRAIT OF A SAVANT, Private collection, New York (*photo:Parke-Bernet*).

Fig. 58. HOLY FAMILY, Private collection, Florence (*photo courtesy Private collection*).

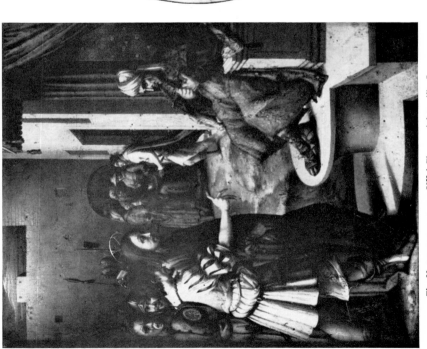

Fig. 60. CHRIST AND PILATE, Uffizi, Florence (photo: Alinari).

Fig. 61. AGONY IN THE GARDEN,
Lycett Green Collection, City of York Art Gallery, England
(photo: courtesy City of York Art Gallery).

Fig. 63. MADONNA AND CHILD WITH THE INFANT ST. JOHN, Gemäldegalerie, Wiesbaden (photo: Gemäldegalerie, Wiesbaden).

Fig. 62. THE HOLY FAMILY IN THE LANDSCAPE, Brescia, whereabouts unknown

Fig. 65. YOUNG ST. JOHN THE BAPTIST,
Collection of Mr. & Mrs. O'Connor Lynch, New York
(photo: courtesy Mr. & Mrs. O'Connor Lynch).

Fig. 64. MADONNA AND CHILD WITH THE INFANT ST. JOHN,
Collection of J. H. van Rooy, the Hague
(photo: reproduced from the "Catalogue of Collection of O. Doetsch, Esq.").

Fig. 66. MADONNA AND CHILD, The Baltimore Museum of Art, Baltimore
(photo: courtesy The Baltimore Museum of Art).

Fig. 67. MADONNA AND CHILD, Collection of Mr. & Mrs. Jack Linsky, New York
(photo: courtesy Mr. & Mrs. Jack Linsky).

Fig. 69. DECAPITATION OF ST. JOHN THE BAPTIST, Staatliche Museen, Berlin
(photo: Staatliche Museen, Berlin).

Fig. 68. HOLY FAMILY, Ambrosiana, Milan (photo: courtesy Ambrosiana).

Fig. 70. MOSES STRIKING THE ROCK, Present whereabouts unknown (*photo: Alinari*).

Fig. 71. THE GATHERING OF MANNA, Bacchiacca, National Gallery of Art, Washington D. C., Samuel H. Kress Foundation (*photo: courtesy National Gallery of Art, Washington, D.C.*).

Fig. 72. MADONNA AND CHILD WITH ST. JOHN, Gemäldegalerie, Dresden
(photo: Gemäldegalerie).

Fig. 74. CONVERSION OF ST. PAUL, The Memorial Art Gallery, of the University of Rochester
(*photo: courtesy The Memorial Art Gallery of the University of Rochester*).

Fig. 75. MARTYRS OF THE ARARAT, S. Firenze, Florence (*photo: Alinari*).

Fig. 76. PORTRAIT OF A LADY, The Springfield Museum of Fine Arts, Springfield, Mass.
(*photo: The Springfield Museum of Fine Arts*).

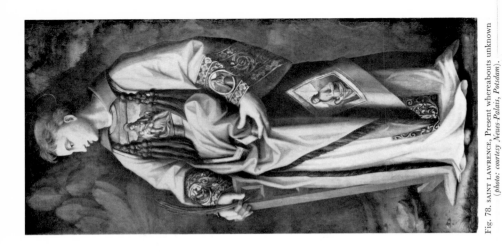

Fig. 78. SAINT LAWRENCE, Present whereabouts unknown
(photo: courtesy Neues Palais, Potsdam).

Fig. 77. SAINT SEBASTIAN, Borgo S. Lorenzo, Mugello (photo: Soprintendenza alle Gallerie).

Fig. 79. MADONNA AND CHILD WITH THE INFANT ST. JOHN, Wildenstein Galleries, New York
(*photo: courtesy Wildenstein Galleries*).

Fig. 80. A FLORENTINE STREET SCENE, Rijksmuseum, Amsterdam (*photo: Rijksmuseum*).

Fig. 81. PORTRAIT OF A LADY IN GREEN,
Present whereabouts unknown (*photo: Parke-Bernet*).

Fig. 82. MADONNA AND CHILD WITH THE INFANT ST. JOHN,
Seminario Patriarcale, Venice (*photo: Alinari*).

Fig. 83. THE FLAGELLATION OF CHRIST,
Umbrian School, c. 1505 National Gallery of Art Washington, D.C.
(*photo: Courtesy National Gallery of Art, Washington, D.C.*).

Fig. 85. PORTRAIT OF THE FLORENTINE LADY,
Present whereabouts unknown
(*photo: reproduced from "Catalogue of Collection of O. Doetsch, Esq."*).

Fig. 87. MARCO CURZIO, The National Gallery, London
(*photo: National Gallery*).